Shrapnel Maps

Also by Philip Metres

Shrapnel Maps
Philip Metres

COPPER CANYON PRESS

PORT TOWNSEND, WASHINGTON

Cover art: Tammam Azzam, *The Place,* photomontage, 2017.
The quotations in the epigraph are from "Rita's Winter" by Mahmoud Darwish in *If I Were Another,* translated by Fady Joudah (Farrar, Straus and Giroux, 2011) and "The Place Where We Are Right" by Yehuda Amichai in *The Poetry of Yehuda Amichai,* edited by Robert Alter (Farrar, Straus and Giroux, 2015).

Copper Canyon Press is in residence at Fort Worden State Park in Port Townsend, Washington, under the auspices of Centrum. Centrum is a gathering place for artists and creative thinkers from around the world, students of all ages and backgrounds, and audiences seeking extraordinary cultural enrichment.

LIBRARY OF CONGRESS CATALOGING-IN-PUBLICATION DATA
Names: Metres, Philip, 1970– author.
Title: Shrapnel maps / Philip Metres.
Description: Port Townsend, Washington : Copper Canyon Press, [2020] |
Identifiers: LCCN 2019043870 | ISBN 9781556595639 (trade paperback)
Subjects: LCSH: Jewish-Arab relations—Poetry. | LCGFT: Poetry.
Classification: LCC PS3613.E887 S57 2020 | DDC 811/.6—dc23
LC record available at https://lccn.loc.gov/2019043870

9 8 7 6 5 4 3 2 FIRST PRINTING

COPPER CANYON PRESS

Post Office Box 271
Port Townsend, Washington 98368
www.coppercanyonpress.org

Acknowledgments

My thanks to the following journals and anthologies for publishing versions of these poems, often with different titles: Academy of American Poets Poem-A-Day, *The American Poetry Review, Arc Poetry Magazine* (Canada), *Barn Owl Review, BathHouse, Beloit Poetry Journal, Bennington Review, Berkeley Poetry Review, Callaloo, The Equalizer, FIELD, Fifth Wednesday Journal, GIANTHOLOGY, Inverted Syntax, Iowa Review, Kenyon Review, The Laurel Review, Matter, Mizna, New American Writing, New England Review, The Normal School, Ostrich Review, POEM* (UK), *The Poetry Project Newsletter, Socialist Review, Southern Indiana Review, Sukoon, Under a Warm Green Linden; Ghost Fishing: An Eco-Justice Poetry Anthology* (University of Georgia, 2018), *Extraordinary Rendition: American Writers on Palestine* (Olive Branch/Interlink, 2016), *Letters to Palestine: Writers Respond to War and Occupation* (Verso, 2015), *Before There Is Nowhere to Stand: Palestine/Israel: Poets Respond to the Struggle* (Lost Horse, 2012), *Come Together: Imagine Peace* (Bottom Dog, 2008).

Returning to Jaffa came out as a chapbook by Diode Editions in 2019. *A Concordance of Leaves* came out as a chapbook by Diode Editions in 2013 and won the Arab American Book Award in 2014. "When It Rains in Gaza" won the Adrienne Rich Award for Poetry in 2019.

Special thanks to Amy Breau, my love, for abiding with me and commenting on many drafts of this book. And to our children, Adele and Leila, for all you are and are becoming. Thanks to Simeon Berry and Chris Kempf for their feedback on multiple drafts. Thanks as well to writers and friends who read versions of these poems: George Abraham, Rebecca Black, Danny Caine, Hayan Charara, Michael Croley, Sarah Gridley, Marwa Helal, Fady Joudah, Ilya Kaminsky, E.J. McAdams, Colum McCann, Katherine Metres, Adam Sol, Phil Terman, Paige Webb, Mary Weems, and Catherine Wing.

Thanks to the whole Copper Canyon Press team: Michael Wiegers, John Pierce, Elaina Ellis, Laura Buccieri, Emily Grise, George Knotek, book designer Phil Kovacevich, copyeditors David Caligiuri and Jessica Roeder, and everyone else who helped bring this book into being.

Thanks to John Carroll University, the Lannan Foundation, and the Ohio Arts Council for their financial support.

Thanks as well to the following artists, scholars, activists, and colleagues from whom I've learned so much: Majed Abbadi, Ali Abu Awwad, Ali Abunimah, Atef Abu Saif, Mosab Abu Toha, Sami Adwan, Kazim Ali, Taha Muhammad Ali, Zaina Alsous, Hala Alyan, Yehuda Amichai, Gish Amit, Huwaida Arraf, Talal Asad, Arik Ascherman, Hanan Ashrawi, Uri Avnery, Ronit Avni, Julia Bacha, Rachel Tzvia Back, Anna Baltzer, Banksy, Daniel Barenboim, Lana Barkawi, Dan Bar-On, Ehud Ben-Ezer, Meron Benvenisti, Noah Bickart, Breaking the Silence, Kathryn Bryan, Emad Burnat, Judith Butler, Noam Chomsky, Peter Cole, Rachel Corrie, Selma Dabbagh, DAM, Robi Damelin, Susan Muaddi Darraj, Mahmoud Darwish, Aaron Davidman, Angela Davis, Manal Deeb, Marcello Di Cintio, Ben Ehrenreich, Noura Erakat, Alan Federman, Norman Finkelstein, Malcolm Fleming, Nahida Halaby Gordon, David Grossman, Emile Habiby, Marilyn Hacker, Samia Halaby, Yossi Klein Halevi, Jeff Halper, Suheir Hammad, Nathalie Handal, Michelle Hartman, Amira Hass, Emily Henochowicz, Matthew Hogan, Jerry Isaak-Shapiro, Annemarie Jacir, Emily Jacir, Khuloud Jaqaman, Randa Jarrar, Rula Jebreal, Kim Jensen, Ghassan Kanafani, Remi Kanazi, Rima Kapitan, Amy Kaplan, Ghada Karmi, Rashid Khalidi, Walid Khalidi, Sahar Khalifeh, Zahi Khamis, Ismail and Abla Khatib, Elias Khoury, Morani Kornberg-Weiss, Michael Lerner, Savyon Liebrecht, Tariq Luthun, Lisa Suhair Majaj, Nur Masalha, Khaled Mattawa, Farid Matuk, Katie Miranda, Jonas Moffat, Ayed Morrar, Iltezam Morrar, Orayb Aref Najjar, Rima Najjar, Ibrahim Nasrallah, Ezra Nawi, Marcy Newman, Naomi Shihab Nye, Mohammed Omer, Ranen Omer-Sherman, Maryvelma Smith O'Neil, Amos Oz, Ilan Pappe, The Parents Circle–Families Forum, Mitri Raheb, Ilana Ratner, Debby Rosenthal, Edward Said, Steven Salaita, Rula Salameh, Rick Schiller, Hanan Schlesinger, Rona Sela, Aharon Shabtai, Erel Shalit, Ari Shavit, Deema Shehabi, Raja Shehadeh, Fazal Sheikh, Adania Shibli, David Shutkin, Nomi Stone, Elia Suleiman, Dareen Tatour, Sandy Tolan, Lena Khalaf Tuffaha, Fadwa Tuqan, Eyal Weizman, S. Yizhar, and Rachel Zolf. These and many others have dedicated themselves to the labor of justice and peace, of reconciliation and liberation. They may differ in their approaches, ideologies, and political aims, but they have taught me something along the way. My words can only share a shadow of their light.

Contents

III. Poster ("Visit Palestine"/Weird Apparition)

IV. Theater of Operations

ACT ONE. OUR HOUSE IS NOW ANOTHER HOUSE

VI. Poster ("Visit") / Unto a Land I Will Show Thee

IX.

X.

The place where we are right
Is hard and trampled
Like a yard.

But doubts and loves
Dig up the world
Like a mole, a plow.
And a whisper will be heard in the place
Where the ruined
House once stood.

Yehuda Amichai

—And about two dreams on the pillow, they intersect and escape so one draws out a
dagger and another entrusts the commandments to the flute

—I don't get the meaning

—Nor do I, my language is shrapnel

Mahmoud Darwish

Shrapnel Maps

I.

One Tree

They wanted to tear down the tulip tree, our neighbors, last year.
It throws a shadow over their vegetable patch, the only tree in our
backyard. We said no. Now they've hired someone to chainsaw an
arm—the crux on our side of the fence—and my wife, in tousled
hair and morning sweats, marches to stop the carnage, mid-limb.
It reminds her of her childhood home, a shady place to hide. She
recites her litany of no, returns. Minutes later, the neighbors emerge.
The worker points to our unblinded window. I want to say, *it's not
me,* slide out of view behind a wall of cupboards, ominous breakfast
table, steam of tea, our two young daughters now alone. I want no
trouble. Must I fight for my wife's desire for yellow blooms when
my neighbors' tomatoes will stunt and blight in shade? Always the
same story: two people, one tree, not enough land or light or love.
As with the baby brought to Solomon, someone must give. Dear
neighbor, it's not me. Bloom-shadowed, light-deprived, they lower
the chainsaw again.

Two Neighbors

In Cleveland, snow so thick it looked as if it were not falling but hovering, I shuffled along the snowbanked side of Washington Boulevard, halfway to campus, when a Suburban scrolled past, slowed. The driver's window lowered to a woman in copper wig. In a Brooklyn accent, she asked if I needed a *roide*. I didn't know her from Eve. She was brave or kind or both. "I'm almost there," I replied. She said, "You'll probably get there before I do!" We laughed together in the falling snow, as she rolled up her window...

Into the minibus, near Jerusalem, the young Palestinian climbed. He wore a pen in his oxford, black hair parted clean. We got to talking where we were from. He hoped, he said, to study engineering in Cleveland. The minivan braked. We pulled out passports. A soldier barked something we couldn't follow, the young man said something we couldn't follow, his hands dancing empty in the air. The soldier grabbed his wrists. We pulled away (we couldn't follow) and he disappeared, surrounded by three soldiers, as we drew near to Jerusalem.

Three Books (A Simultaneity)

Readers of columns one and three can repeat every line as they descend the page.

1.	2.	3.
May you be written	once was a book so large	we lived in those leaves
	you couldn't behold it—	
we say, inscribed	you'd have to march	before we were torn
	for miles just to read a line,	
into the Book of Life		
		scissored from branch
	the ink so richly black	
According to Talmud	it felt like falling just to look	
	and each stanza was not a room	shorn from the spine
there is another book	but a state, and each poem	
		again, every day
for the wicked: inscribed		
	a country of its own…	
	Some days we could not tell	we won't give up
	what was the poem	
and sealed for death,	and what was the world	this binding
and a third for those		
	When we felt the breeze,	again, every day
in between the books	we wondered whether	
	it was someone turning a leaf	probing its book
	or a new season's weather	
where most of us live		
	We could spend our life	seeking the binding
suspended, trying	like this, walking the page,	
	waking each new line,	again, every day
not to be swallowed	and never be the same	
		the yet-unscribed
	Yes, the sky was the sky,	where we are
by the past,	and the land was the land,	
	but we had to find	the leaves
dismembered by future,	where the book ended	
praying to be written	and where we begin	writing ourselves back

No man can stand here by deserted Ain Mellahah and say the prophecy has not been fulfilled.

In a verse from the Bible which I have quoted above, occurs the phrase "all these kings." It attracted my attention in a moment, because it carries to my mind such a vastly different significance from what it always did at home. I can see easily enough that if I wish to profit by this tour and come to a correct understanding of the matters of interest connected with it, I must studiously and faithfully unlearn a great many things I have somehow absorbed concerning Palestine. I must begin a system of reduction. Like my grapes which the spies bore out of the Promised Land, I have got everything in Palestine on too large a scale. Some of my ideas were wild enough. The word Palestine always brought to my mind a vague suggestion of a country as large as the United States. I do not know why, but such was the case. I suppose it was because I could not conceive of a small country having so large a history. I think I was a little surprised to find that the grand Sultan of Turkey was a man of only ordinary size. I must try to reduce my ideas of Palestine to a more reasonable shape. One gets large impressions in boyhood, sometimes, which he has to fight against all his life. "All these kings." When I used to read that in Sunday-school, it suggested to me the several kings of such countries as England, France, Spain, Germany, Russia, etc., arrayed in splendid robes ablaze with jewels, marching in grave procession, with scepters of gold in their hands and flashing crowns upon their heads. But

214

II.

A Concordance of Leaves

ورق

(

because he drove the highway north, as if across
the pages of   Caesarea / Nazareth / Galilee—

(

Rami, sunglassed cabbie born in al-Quds, dead ringer
for Travolta circa *Saturday Night Fever*

(

lost the way from Ben Gurion / in jammed
Israeli traffic he called out in Hebrew to unknown

(

cousins in cars / so close you could share
a kiss / asking for directions to Hadera

(

nearest our destination / not our destination,
our destination outside their map of kin & ken—

ورق

(

& because we swam in traffic for hours
lost / lapping Haifa twice / my bladder

(

began to ache / before the highway
split he pulled off / I bouldered hillside

(

until barbed wire & unknown tower
& pissed, half in ecstasy, half in terror

(

a sniper's bullet would chauffeur me
from this place—pants undone, penis in hand—

(

all I could hear was wind / wind beneath the passing
rush hour, older than the rocks I darkened—

ورق

(

on drying racks tobacco leaves swim
wind turns the pages of the book

(

we can only read in the rough translation
of my soon-to-be brother-in-law

(

& this is the brother of my soon-to-be
brother-in-law, inhaling through the straw

(

of his cigarette: holds it between ring
& middle fingers, palm up: the unseen

(

& inaccessible sea caresses our strange faces—
blind & we wait for our lines to be read

ورق

(

& this is the cemetery, where the father
of his father's father's father's father's

(

father's buried, bodies marked by broken
stone incisors, among neighbors

(

we sip sage tea, *maramia*—named after
the mother of God—for sage slaked her

(

desert tongue & now a cousin comes, footfalls
lifting white dust from the mouth

(

of that abandoned quarry, its jurassic cranes
& rusted conveyors hauling nothing, now:

ورق

    (

the last time you rose from the bed
of hills & swales, sister you left

    (

your new love at Tel Aviv, history
holding him at passport control—he passed

    (

an olive tree necklace to you saying
a country is more important than one person

    (

you'd carry its quandary ten years
around your wandering

    (

& now this country draws you
the way olive roots welcome far water

ورق

(

sister soon you will be written
alongside your future

(

husband in the book of books
& though our father's passport

(

held aloft on the only road
will not stop the Sabra tank

(

you will find another way
through rutted olive

(

orchards & soon new sisters
will soften your feet with oil

ورق

(

of barbed wire I clear a line
sharp enough to ribbon the flesh

(

& the village, where Omar nests
in his palm a bird whose wing is broken

(

he strokes & holds to his lips
coffee with cardamom & the circle of men:

(

all day, nearby, some machine putts
as if trying to set the whole village to

(

motion: it won't start
but something is happening, or will:

ورق

    (

& our family will ask so many questions we will
be called The Question Factory

    (

& you my future brother will write your answers
with my slowly disappearing hand

    (

The Question Factory asks: what is a dunam?
Answer: *slowly disappearing land*

    (

The Question Factory asks: what is that line
on your skull? Answer: *a failed poem*

    (

by one who tries to write over everything
already scratched out, written over

ورق

(

The Question Factory: why do you smile?
because I still have my teeth

(

: where are the doll's missing eyes?
in the back of my mind I believe

(

: in what?
I believe I hear a song

(

: why do you laugh?
because I still have my tongue

(

there is a song, & yet
I hear no singing

ورق

Today	اليوم *el youm*
My friend	صديقي *sadiqi*
Sweet/Beautiful	حلاوة *halwa*
Tree	شجرة *shajarah*
Forbidden [shame]	حَرَام *haram*
My name is	اسمي *ismi*
Listen	اسمع *isma'*
It means	يعني *y'anni*
Here	هنا *han*

زيتون

(

consider the olive: it gnarls as it grows
into itself / a veritable thicket / it throws

(

up obstacles to the light to reach
the light / a crooked path in the air

(

while beneath our sight it wrestles the rock
wrests water from whatever trickles

(

beneath / it doesn't worry it looks like hell
refuses to straighten for anyone

(

each spring offers itself / meat to be eaten
first brambles / then olives

ورق

(

for throwing a Molotov at a bus, Muhammed
spent a month his head buried in burlap

(

now my new brother cradles his skull / his bulk
tiptoes the new house no doors on the frames

(

nowhere & nothing to hide / he sweeps all the noise
with insistent silence & hands tied in knots of not

(

knowing what to do with suddenness
now his wife Amal & her black eyes gleam

(

in the dark room—to her breast she quiets
Carmel, which means "God's vineyard"

ورق

(

scarved sisters are radiant with wide
mouths & waves & teeth & singing

(

& though there is the great unhappiness
framed in silent unsmiling faces

(

hammered on insides of houses
watching over all preparations

(

night is lifting the women
are drumming the tabla their voices inviting

(

a heart to break itself & open
a space another could nest inside

ورق

)

because there is a word for love in this tongue
that entwines two people as one

)

& there is a word for love in this tongue
that nests in the chambers of the heart

)

& a word for love in this tongue that wanders
the earth, for love in this tongue in which you lose

)

yourself in this tongue & a word that carries
sorrow within its vowels & a word for love

)

that exudes from your pores & a word
for love that shares its name with falling

ورق

)

& though a careless assistant
will enter the darkroom unbidden

)

& burn the wedding negatives
something larger than wave hovers

)

& buoys us in its wake, large as the sun
as it breaks into hills as if coaxed by the singers

)

to hold another's shoulder or hand off our hands
to another & sway our branches

)

& stamp the dear earth so hard it feels
we are lifting together / its trembling chest

ورق

)

& having been warned to tell the truth
& nothing but the truth

)

I, the undersigned, do hereby swear
the sun-cured page

)

of each tobacco leaf awaits
to be crushed & burned into lungs

)

each olive tree has a thousand eyes
that ripen into sight

)

& the pomegranates of Toura
are planets

ورق

)

If to Bethlehem we must pass through Wadi al-Nar

)

If your license plates are painted blue & black

)

If your permit permits no passage across bypass highways

)

If from a distance the road carves alephs or alifs

)

If no-man's-land is where men live who have no land

)

If you lower your sunshield & block the hilltop settlement

)

If Wadi al-Nar is the Valley of Fire

)

If we must travel beneath the level of our eventual grave

)

If we arrive & they ask *how are you*, we are to say *thank God*

ورق

)

& though the border guard will advise us
this is a dangerous time to visit

)

& though we had to lie & say we were tourists
& not guests at our sister's wedding

)

to spare ourselves the special interrogation
in Ben Gurion / & beyond the wall

)

emerge blinking into the light of a modern Oz
blooming with sprinklered English lawns

)

the dancers in their purple spangled parachute
pants will turn wheels in the dust until the dust

ورق

)

is a violet fire & though the checkpoints hunker
in bunkers & Uzis with Uzis will raise them

)

at our unwitting arrival & cause us to lower
cameras & though hawkers hawk songbirds

)

at Qalandia checkpoint where empty bags tumble
free between the fences of No-Man's-Land

)

& the lines of the people are mute with waiting
the *ataaba* singers will arrive in the village

)

& name-check our families *marhaba Metres
marhaba / marhaba Abbadi marhaba*

ورق

)

& though some seaside café will split into glassy
shards of people these people

)

will have had nothing to do
with it, the bulldozers will doze their roads

)

so that every road ends in a wall
every car will off-road through olive groves

)

& though we won't see the sea the wind
will haul it & the whole village will arrive

)

at the village, until the village will be
a living map of itself, actual size

ورق

)

& though there is a boy whose cheek
is a scar & no father, his eyes like broken eggs

)

the children will flock to every flat roof
to watch the village become the village

)

& see the wedding from enough distance
it looks like a story that could be entered

)

& see the men pin paper money to the suit
of the groom, until he's feathered with future

)

& though everyone will eat, & eat again,
some miracle of lambs

ورق

)

& though the bride's arms & legs will itch
with arabesques & scripts

)

a second skin won't be scratched away
& though her mother will be angry

)

the women & children will wait
until all the men have been served

)

& even the bride plays a role she only
learns on hennaed heels

)

& though tradition is an invisible
author only the old hands hear

ورق

)

& though the sun will be too bright for the bride
to see beyond her own eyes

)

& though the bullet in the groom will begin
to hatch in his side, & the stitches in his skull

)

will singe another verse in the book of dreams,
& though the bride's questions will beak their shells

)

years from now, now, now let there be dancing
in circles, let the village become arms flung

)

drawing bodies to bodies & let heads nod
& eyes widen, which we translate as meaning:

ورق

Accept this…	تفضل *tfaddul*
Congratulations	مبروك *mabrouk*
How much?	قديش بدك *addaish badak?*
I don't understand	انا مش فاهم *ana mish fahim*
Tomorrow	بكرا *bukra*
Apricots	مشمش *mishmish*
Tomorrow, when the apricots ripen	بكرا في المشمش *bukra fil mishmish*
Tomorrow never comes	بكرا في المشمش *bukra fil mishmish*
Ready?	يلّا *yallah?*
Let's go	يلّا *yallah*

ورق

)

you my sister you my brother
outside the walls / in the wind

)

if Aristophanes was right
& we walk the world

)

in search of, a split-
infinitive of *to love*, if two .

)

outside the walls / in the wind
we should sing

)

outside the walls / in the wind
you my sister you my brother

)

outside the walls / in the wind
& let *our eccho ring:*

Coda

like strapping a small bomb
to your third finger / that ring

)

about which we could not
speak upon our arrival

)

& departure from the country
of memory where we left you

)

sister / among the fragile
projectiles inside the book

)

whose pages the wind riffles
searching for a certain passage

III.

THE TOURIST OFFICE OF THE JEWISH AGENCY FOR PALESTINE JERUSALEM

Arabs, agonizing and infernal chorus
Arabs, all in ragged, sooty, soiled, and scanty raiment
Arabs, buxom girls with repulsively tattooed lips and chins
Arabs, cadaverous
Arabs, crew of filthy
Arabs, dusky faces and strange costumes
Arab, feet are not clean and smells like a camel
Arab, ferocious
Arab, fine looking
Arab, fringed and bedizened prince
Arab, howling dervishes and hundreds of breeds of
Arabs, idling about
Arab, masquerading
Arab, perched on a camel
Arabs, quarrelling like cats and dogs
Arab, saluting
Arab, scowling
Arabs, sore-eyed children
Arabs, swarm of uncouth
Arabs, tents
Arabs, vermin-coated vagabonds
Arab, weird apparition
Arab, wild

Visit
PALESTINE
SEE ANCIENT BEAUTY REVIVED

Our Quiet Saturdays

for Jerry Isaak–Shapiro

You know Richard Pryor, the black comedian,
used the N-word until he went to Nairobi?

Seeing black people in charge of the country—
from the wino to the president—changed him.

Damn, I thought, *he's talking about Zionism.*
Because that's how American Jews feel, like him,

walking in wonder on the streets in Israel,
our quiet Saturdays. At last, we have a home!

Anti-Semitism, intermarriage: my friends tell
me I'm crazed, always worrying. Easy for them.

When there are sixty million Jews in this country
then we won't worry about every single family.

So when you get to a place that's the only place
you're in the majority, you see it differently.

Innocents Abroad (II)

~~Others were Baptists, seeking Baptist evidences and a Baptist Palestine. Others were Catholics, Methodists, Episcopalians, seeking evidences indorsing their several creeds, and a Catholic, a Methodist, an Episcopalian Palestine. Honest as these men's intentions may have been, they were full of partialities and prejudices,~~ they entered the country with their verdicts already prepared, ~~and they could no more write dispassionately and impartially about it than they could about their own wives and children. Our pilgrims have brought their verdicts with them.~~ They have shown ~~it in their conversation ever since we left Beirut. I can almost tell, in set phrases, what they will say when they see Tabor, Nazareth, Jericho, and Jerusalem—because I have the books they will "smouch" their ideas from. These authors will~~ pictures and ~~frame~~ rhapsodies, and ~~leave men follow and~~ see with the author's eyes instead of their own, and speak with his tongue. ~~What the pilgrims said at Cesarea Philippi surprised me with its wisdom. I found it afterwards in Robinson. What they said when Genessaret burst upon their vision charmed me with its grace. I find it in Mr. Thompson's "Land and the Book." They have spoken often, in happily-worded language which never varied, of how they meant to~~ lay their weary heads upon ~~a stone at Bethel as Jacob did, and close their dim eyes, and dream, perchance, of angels descending out of heaven on a ladder. It was very pretty. But I have recognized the weary head and the~~ dim eyes,

IV.
Theater of Operations

In memory of Noah, Ghassan, Nachom, Jamil, Yael, Tariq, Salim, Adina, Karim, Avi, Ibrahim, Azriel, Rachel, Ayat & Ahmed

Act One. Our House Is Now Another House

I. NOAH

The chush of hydraulic breaks, squall of the door
& I'm in it. Among my people. My people

busing off to work, school, shop, see the doctor.
I search their faces. So this is Home. Is it possible

they take these asphalted ways through the Torah
& don't think Torah? O Israel. Like in a dream,

I sit beside the mirror of my father's mother,
lost in the Holocaust, the ones that we redeem.

She's knitting a shawl small enough for a child,
another finger in Hitler's eye. No, a child

who will laugh without fear. But why am I still afraid
of this Arab here? My tongue wrestles with new words—

so why do I taste metal, like blood in the mouth?
Why do I feel so alive, this close to death?

2. GHASSAN

In the other room, in Beirut, you asked your mother:
"am I a Palestinian?" She paused. Said *yes*—

& a heavy silence fell over the house, as if
something hanging above our heads had fallen. Later,

I heard you crying. I couldn't move. In the other room
you gave birth to yourself. A blessèd scalpel opened

your chest & inserted this heart, the distant homeland
rising inside: the terraced walls & hills around al-Quds,

the orange orchards of Jaffa, Haifa's salt-sweet air,
dry musk of sage & thyme in wadis, groves of olive

& tobacco in Jenin, names wrapped in white cloth
& held above the head. We are born so fast—a word,

in a moment, begins a new throb. A name hurls
us from the ceiling of childhood onto the road.

3. NACHOM

like Russian roulette / a circle you don't know
whether you will / be inside the next time

I have only this / unexploded moment /
where the future crouches / a burning smell /

& yet / what is nested inside the buzz
of living / to sleepwalk your kids to school

& at the café break open / a croissant
cup of coffee / flirt with the barista

then on Sabbath arise to see the street
go quiet / & the day draw wide / & wider /

a whole country on pause / this Jewish life /
I have told you only half / of what I

fear / this moment where past huddles / if I hear
a car backfire / door slam / balloon pop / I jump

4. JAMIL

each day I enter with open / papers & snake the coiled
wires & barbed cattle chute / Qalandia / & bunker sand

-bagged heads / to study the very ground / & watch oneself
being watched / a ticking watch / other's hands handing over

to red-haired & fretting / Uzi itchy with questions
& half a world / from his birth / a passportless plastic bag

scuds & tumbles past border / its blue flag blessed by wind /
O to be winged / & not locked in the fate of checkpoints

outside the milk of oxygen / held up / outside the /
in / no man's / land / to lift outside gravity's root & float

in the matrix / the mind a stone / bones grinding themselves
like teeth / in this mouth / vacuum-locked / suspended

till he gloves back / the papers / aviators glinting back
this alien's alien face

5. YAEL

in the Bible there's no West Bank no Green Line no
Occupied Territory / just where forefathers

lived & we want to live & pray / so my father
began the archaeological dig / Shiloh /

first outpost / & then people began to move here
to fulfill the covenant / to take what's ours

study scripture / pray under Abraham's heavens /
on a bus to Tel Aviv to protest the "peace"

my friend's mother was shot & killed / she left seven
children / seven children / at last I understood

someone will want always to kill us / to erase
us again & now we say we will not let them

& in the mountain's fold / touched by her blood
the foundation we shall build

6. TARIQ

they say they own this land / a paper that says
they own / we have papers that go further back

we wait for them / any moment they can
evict us / my sisters had to leave the house

my father is afraid / & our house is now
another house / not the house we used to live in

house we grew up in / internationals
living with us / we're not together anymore

my father since forty days / at any moment
my sister at grandmother's / trying to stay

strong but inside they tremble / & whisper
to friends / waiting for / a story in the paper

nights I play poker / it's not what you have
but what you make them think you have

7. SALIM

To lift my arms as if in praise / when they strap it beneath
my shirt, to feel the ice-cold shell / against my chest, its promised

hatching into blood-heat. To imagine myself already
dead, yet buoy in the wash / of capillaries pulsing like web,

every strand tensile, agleam. To tread the streets now paved
over my father's house & to be held / up at the checkpoint

between my village & what's left / of our groves of lemon
& olive—razor-wired & identity card. To believe that

this will stanch his wound, this mad algebra dividing
all numbers back to one, the columns on each side

of the equal sign equal again, if I can walk into a stranger's café
& in a sudden illumination / join shard to skin, flesh

to flesh, & wake us / from a nightmare, unhooked
from the wall like a clock / that needs to be wound again.

Act Two. This Tide of Blood

I. ADINA

First the sudden / deaf as in a dream / people & their mouths
open & moving not sounding out. / Plaster & glass dress.

Frame of the face frozen in & you running. In place.
This was my store, my plate / glass, my café, turned in

-side out. What is tumble & shard? You see your mouth
before you hear it, wax of the explosion now unplugged

& bleeding ear. Smoke the mouth / the door. Everything now
shaken, the salt of plaster & sliver no time

to make of this anything but the rubble of the human.
& where are you, the one I love, who serves everyone—

That is not your leg. Bloodslick & shatter. Is there nothing,
no clock to wake us from this dream? I'm standing

in someone else's brain.
My love, I have no mouth.

2. KARIM

My job was to disappear. To follow orders in another
hard tongue & hold / my own. / My job: to clear

the tables of the leavings, to harvest the crumbs,
to shoot / the plates with so much scalding water

I could see my unshaven / face in them. / To plumb
the overflowing toilet, that constant fountain

of other people's shit, I had to breathe through
my mouth & curse this lot. I couldn't help myself

to what others could not eat—it touched their mouths
& lingered against their lips, which cursed the wealth

of my slowness when I did not hear their call or heard
their hidden distaste. So when he sat down,

his eyes darting, I knew this was my chance
to choose my fate / to end / my disappearance—

3. AVI & IBRAHIM (A CHORUS)

It's because I wanted it to happen. Longed & waited.
Let there be flash & flood, I said, let there be black

& acrid, choking lungs. I said, yes, send
rivulets of red, plaster in the scalp, democratic,

& dark hovering over the surfaces of everything.
Let there be klieg lights & sudden cameramen & lens

& cordons policing the scene, the secular expanse
of a café now sacred by blood. & let us sing

this memorial to the lost, this blessèd loneliness—
let there be blood to remind our people who we are

& what we have suffered at the gloves of our oppressor,
those long & desolate years, our lips probing a font

from a rock. To remember that this is nothing if not war,
& in this tide of blood we all get what we want.

4. AZRIEL

for Zaka

Because someone has to pick up the pieces
of G-d. We get the call & don neon vests

to sort the flesh from flesh. There is a kindness
in looking. To bring even a finger to burial.

Here is a human bomb. Here is a wedding hall.
Now scrape the bride & groom gently from the walls.

They scatter higher—onto trees, roofs, balconies.
A ladder to gather them up, to put them together

like a puzzle. Something pushes them to do this.
No matter what they have done, each human

in the image of G-d. A baby strapped in a stroller
ID'd by the stroller. There is a kindness.

Everybody wants his company to grow.
May HaShem help us go out of business.

5. [BREAKING NEWS]

struck a shopping street in / attacked
a bakery in / himself & three people, police said

in a pool hall / himself up outside a fast food
in a retaliation / killing him before he could

so long as there is / there will be / so long
as there is / there will be / in retaliation

radio said missiles / claimed responsibility
said showering glass / said man without legs

said narrow alleys / said half the wall fell on them
struck / & in retaliation for in retaliation

ten people / & dozens of others / violations
will be met / in revenge for / will halt

in revenge / as soon as / & dozens of others
will be met / said crowded busy / said half the wall

6. GIDON

I wanted to sit across / to go in / more depth
plumb their souls / look them / in the eye / see if they look

me in the eye / note their expression when I ask
them "why" / face / to face how I would feel / to know

what causes a person to go out & murder
because you know / I've been at the scenes just after

& I don't have words for it / & now this / this thing
before me constantly her eyes / dart / reciting

the brainwashing / but she can't tell me anything
that can explain / just a system & a satanic

aim / they say: I die, therefore I live / I listen
well / gather intel / "know thy enemy"

they home in like a spider & spin /
a virtual world / the rest doesn't interest me

7. SAHAR

for reason not / totally clear / I was to wear
tight pants midriff shirt & congratulations a backpack

of blood / to be with him in Paradise / with Salim
so fast I never imagined it could happen so fast

to be reunited in heaven a real heroine / I did
whatever they told me / I was thinking only of him

I got out of the car / the place not exactly
like on the map / lot of people, mothers with / re-

membered / an Israeli girl I used to / Facebook
before / I looked at the faces / I looked at the clouds

& walking toward the pizza shop I smelled the thyme
& then I caught my own reflection in the glass

& then I understood what I was about
to do / & now I'm here / & the fact is: I didn't

Act Three. The Matter of the Flesh of One's Flesh

I. MIRIAM

at shore's edge I watch a mother holding vigil
surf detonating against the sand / her toddler

hobwobbles as if his legs were stumps or numb
the tide tugs his feet / he bends to test its chaos

to grasp & grapple with ungraspable silver
ever-breaking mirror / offering to swallow

the magnet-shimmer & rupture of salt-white froth
drawing him in / she won't let her / eyes meander

& so much like my son so much like myself
on this same beach years before the detonation

there is the matter of the flesh of one's flesh
& its audacity to wander unhindered

as if blind to its ten thousand tethers / all stitched
into his mother's breast / she's waiting for the pull

2. MARYAM

I don't care what he did. His body came from my body.
After the crashing, after the pushing, the waves of pain,

they cut the cord between us, & I brought him to my breast.
With his small mouth, without words, he called the milk out of me.

When we had nothing to drink but the salt of the sea, rain
was our dream. We slept under tin & stone & had no rest.

First rain, then missiles, then Cobras & drones overhead.
Then soldiers thundering the alleys, flooding front doors

in the middle of the night. Seeing his own brother dead,
then wrapped in winding cloth, lifted high by sudden strangers.

We carry the keys & deeds in our chests & heads, how we fled
the village they bulldozed to rubble but could not erase

from maps we nursed inside. He tried to bring that map to life.
I could not stop him. I did what I could to keep him safe.

3. AARON

My flesh has swallowed an entire dream of heaven:
I've got a dozen screws floating around my spine,

casings & shells, mortar & construction nails
holding nothing forever. For legs I wheel

this chair. My body's locked in the pitying gaze
of strangers, family, in the moment he froze

our fates together. I recall trying to rise,
slipping as if on ice, unseeing my eyes,

my father's voice screaming something—what was my name—
but I could only see his mouth moving, the pain

in his eyes. I could not feel a thing. Every day
I try to stand again. Sometimes I'm filled with joy,

sometimes I want to die. Myself I devour.
For his wish to be remembered, I'm raked with fire.

4. RACHEL & AYAT (A CHORUS)

my name was Rachel I listened
our bodies found on opposite

to Pink Floyd & Christina Aguilera
my name was Ayat I watched

ends of the café / the television
intifada on Al Jazeera

around the face of the dead / martyr
murderer / they make the frame

around the face of the victim / victim
oppressor / we break the frame

ourselves / at first they could not tell
our dark bodies apart

my name was Ayat I watched
my name was Rachel I listened

5. ISMAIL & ABLA TO AHMED, THEIR SON

your body full / of fragments / harrowed was thy brain
spilled over your clothes / you / already not

of this world / in the shadow of our difficult / we plant
your heart inside / a teenaged girl you will

never touch / liver we bury / in a baby you will
never raise / elderly you'll never be / kidneys

we resettle in alien skin / your lungs now breathe
for two who could not breathe without you

we know your toy gun looked / death
in the eye but why / did they have to shoot you

twice / & now inside "the enemy" you rise
behind the lines of inside / you live

& see for yourself what none of us can see
ourselves / ourselves from the outside

6. AN INDEX

With scissors & Samson, see. With columns,
see, see also. With gunpowder, my liege.

With rusted nail heads, see. With ball bearings,
see. With broken razors & razor wire, page.

With darts, seized. & screws, see. & with shrapnel.
With pipe casings, seamed. C-4. See rage.

On foot, page. By explosive belt, see. Satchel
charge, see. & also see. By car & by cage.

By submarine, sea. In the flesh, see. By mule,
page. By baby carriage. By bicycle, see. By plane.

With shard & with shell. Innovations
of projectile. Asymmetrical, viz. edged.

For disambiguation, see Mother of Satan.
Cf. skin to kin.

7. CHORUS

lig ht with   outhe at   wo   rd w   ithout le   afw   ear   e

sh   ad   owsofse   l v e s   nol   ong   erlo   cke   din

bo   dies   werest   in thef   old of so   met   hing

likefur a s   hared s   kin   li   ght without ey   ewords

wit   h   out m out   h   h   ear   here   youth   ere s   t   ill   l   iving

int   he sha   d   owof   s   elf   rig   hte   ousne   ss

wef   lo   at ab   ove   youn   olo   ngerb   a   lance

on   thes   h   rap   nel   ed   geo   f   ma   ps

wew   ho   h   ave & no   lon   ge   rke   epk   eys

to go   ne h   ou   sesw   e who h   ave & nolon   gerc   up thesp   layed

ner   ves o   fanc   es   torsweh   ave & nolon   g   er unf   url

the c   oil of in   herit   edc   odes   weno   longercar   ry on

thist   heat   er of d   is   re   m   e m   ber   thisf   east

ofg   rief   can   no tnot   re   mi   ndy   o   u   w   e

V.

~~Temple stood. This Mosque is the holiest place the Mohammedan knows, outside of Mecca. Up to within a year or two past no Christian could gain admission to it or its court for love or money. But the prohibition has been removed, and we entered freely for backsheesh.~~

~~I need not speak of~~ the wonderful beauty and the exquisite grace and symmetry that have made this ~~Mosque so celebrated—because~~ I did not see ~~them.~~ One cannot see ~~such things at a single glance—one frequently only finds out~~ how really beautiful a really beautiful woman is after considerable acquaintance with ~~her; and the rule applies to Niagara Falls, to majestic mountains, and to mosques—especially to mosques.~~

~~The great feature of the Mosque of Omar is the prodigious rock in the center of its rotunda. It was upon~~ this rock ~~that Abraham came so near offering up his son Isaac—this, at least, is authentic—is is very much more to be relied on than most of the traditions, at any rate. On~~ this rock, ~~also, the angel stood and threatened Jerusalem, and David persuaded him to spare the city. Mahomet was well acquainted with this stone. From it he ascended to heaven. The stone tried to follow him, and if the angel Gabriel had not happened by the merest good luck to be there to seize it, it would have done it. Very few people have a grip like Gabriel—the prints of his monstrous fingers, two inches deep, are to be seen in that rock to-day.~~

The Tel Rumeida Circus for Detained Palestinians

for Jonas Moffat and Katie Miranda

And though this scorched earth gives birth to a stone
for every stone that's thrown, Jonas can cast

three stones into the air, to hover there;
and though Jamil has lost his sense of smell,

because he lifts his gaze to the gyres
of poi fire—the tension of detention

turns to attention; and when Katie turns
the flares around her, as if she were trapped

in the center of ignition, unburned,
Palestinians lined at the checkpoint

laugh with the soldiers who check their papers,
who won't invent their own entertainment—

like make an old man kiss his donkey's ass—
when these American clowns swallow fire.

According to This Midrash

for Rabbi Arik Ascherman

The midrash says, when Hagar and Ishmael are banished
into the desert, before God builds a well, the angels

cry, "What are you doing? Don't you know the tsuris
the Jewish people are going to suffer at the hands

of the children of Ishmael?" And God, according to this midrash,
says, "Right now, in front of me, there's a child. Right now

this child is innocent." Look, I know some Palestinians
would want to kill me and my children. I know some Israelis

do not see Palestinians as human, and use the law
to keep us separate. But when I visit Palestinians, they waken

their children to meet us, in the caves where they live
after their house was demolished. We sit on packed suitcases

as they serve me tea. Their son who'd been tied to a windshield
by the army, and the man in a kippa who'd come to his aid.

The Dance of the Activist and the Typist

for Huwaida Arraf, blocking a soldier from
shooting demonstrators

she inserts the inked ribbon of herself
between the black roller of history

and the alphabetic metal legs
of that inverted insect—rifles

thrash the air the targets / scatter / she can't
help it / something in her / grows each time she turns

to face the rifle / grows as she covers
its permanent erection / the typist

lifts his wrists / and legs hover to stamp /
where the rifle moves, she moves / a mirror

following the lead of inevitable
lead / she's the rifle / unfired / shield of flesh

her arms overhead / before the muzzle
as if she could cradle a bullet

VI.

Unto a Land I Will Show Thee

Now the LORD had said unto Abram, Get thee out of thy country, and from thy kindred, and from thy father's house, unto a land I will shew thee

Genesis 12:1

Palestinae sive totius Terrae Promissionis nova descriptio

Seven years we lived with this map, bought at a garage sale to fill a wall in our new house. As Orthodox neighbors sauntered by that Saturday toward Young Israel of Greater Cleveland, our baby slept car-seated in the moving truck, and we populated the house with our belonging, afraid to move her and wake her up.

We lusted for each other like chaste unmarrieds, our baby fitful between us. Day and dark, beneath our night-shadowed eyes, the sleepless comma fattened with milk. Somehow, we lived.

Seven years. Still sleepless. A second baby now at your breast, I walk the midnight house. The living room. I'd never looked close enough to see

[near a masted vessel

in bed my body   your body inviting

[toward the shore of the Holy
[familiar curve of the land spooning the sea

nursing the child between us

Love, this place we've found
ourselves lost   [unfurling cartouche

I brush

your spine, signing

[The column of brushed-brown vertebrae, signifying

Palestine or the new description of the Promised Land

[   ]

In the Heights, we calculate the statistical risk of greeting strangers, memorize geometry of eyes. Study arabesques in concrete sidewalk slabs as we draw closer to or farther from temples on opposite ends of our town: Catholic and Jewish. Greet the stranger gingerly, as if our words could bruise or batter. Down the street from the old Jewish orphanage—which, last century, the city once denied a permit— outside my home, I say hello and my neighbors look right through me, as if I can't be seen, or they say hello and surprise me out of my silence. "I like your sign," a woman nods, pointing to our placard: *In this house we believe… kindness is everything*. Assonance of Sabbaths side by side, we scan the prosodies of hemline and headgear, imagery of unveiled front room windows, stanzas where we display the wares of our faith, as if on sale, hoping our enormous gods will notice, lean down, and scoop us up.

Palestinae [Rudimentum Novit[i]orum] [1475]

Palestine (Attempt by novices)?

  Let me be clear, the ambassador stated, *Palestine does not exist in the Bible.*

        Watch this, you said.

           Split-screen videos, two
           presidents emerging
           from limousines
           eight years apart. One
           waits, turning to his wife

Palestine (Attempt to reconstitute)?

  It was a Roman invention to ensure the elimination of the Jews.

        See how he waits

          his right hand delicate
          on the small of her back
          as she rises up the stairs.

          The other man bombs
          ahead, his blonde
          trailing, forgotten. The one

Palestine?
  There is no such thing as a Palestinian.

        Now look at this guy

          we detest is the one
          who reminds me

          of me

[   ]

My neighbor's handshake is firm, his black kippa's clipped close to his scalp, hair ruffling in the wind. With plastic rake, I'm scaring the final evidence of fall from my drive. *So why can't my daughter play at your house with your daughter?* I say, trying to understand. His smile winces. *My wife,* he says, *she grew up only around our kind.* I look away, not wanting to salt the pain. *I think we're generous to others,* he says, trying to explain. *Not like the Arabs.* Looking back up, I see the redheaded soldier at a West Bank checkpoint my Arab father engaged in conversation. *You're from Brooklyn, what are you doing here?*—each of them could have asked the other. My checkered keffiyeh hangs in the closet, visible only to me. White flakes descend. He talks around the awkwardness. I scrape the last dead leaves. The Arab in me still wants to invite him in for tea. The American in me wants the Arab to turn and disappear in the falling snow.

[Fill in the Blanks: Adele's Sunday School Homework]

ISRAEL

Directions: Use your Bible and the clues on the "Places in the Holy Land" worksheet to help you fill in the blanks on the map below.

Activity 3: Fill in the Blank Map of Israel

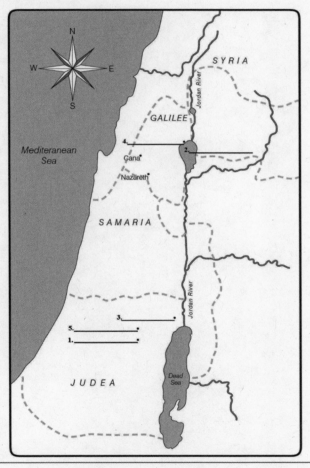

The Holy Land Franciscans

79

Is most true and the most considerable of all for the entire Land of promise, from
Dan even to Beersheba, a description of the

As with a map, as with narrative

Any chosen detail necessarily blots out

Proximate details

You just don't listen,
She says, shaking her head

You only hear
What you already believe

Look at me,
She says

What do you want
To see

Say: that painted copse of trees

A quaint flourish

Covers a village

[   ]

The road from mouth to ear narrows at once, stops at checkpoints for identification. Walls you can't see until you run into them—as at night, a guest wanders a dark house. In our bed, you say: *you talk all day of dialogue between Palestinians and Israelis, of being open, but right now, in our own house, you can't hear me.* My tongue is a key broken in its lock.

What our neighbor Ari saw: the blind and deaf Israelis of Nalagaat stand before a table, mix invisible flour with invisible water, roll out a dough, and gather it to a loaf. One says: *when someone touches my hand, I can feel my loneliness start to disappear.* The dance of his hands, bidding the beautiful to rise.

Ari, a doctor, asked me to print his theater tickets on Sabbath. We talked Chekhov, how he beheld everyone—in "Ward No. 6," the pitiable Jew who begged for kopecks, the cynical doctor who justified his failures, the insane patient who caused the doctor to question everything.

In the dark again, you: *you don't let me in. You'd rather face a checkpoint in another country than let me in.* What stops me from opening like the neighbor's maple, every inch of it turning to light? You're asleep now, prone in your dream. I rise, wander the pitch-dark rooms of our house, holding out my hands.

[   ]

the very act of [   ] a thing with edges

I had a hand in producing the [   ]
and no idea what I was doing

late one night my commander
led me to a room

and piles of [   ] everywhere
handed me a dried-out marker

unfurled a [   ] I'd never seen before
me to trace certain lines and shapes

just make them clearer, he said

a geo-body   the shape of

Arafat glared at the [   ] in silence
"You want me to accept *cantons?*

You want to *destroy* me."
with edges a body and the necessity

of defending

[   ]

Not a box. A large jar, usually of rough-grained terra-cotta, used for storage.

She asks, *Why can't I go into Yael's house?*

Cf. Hesiod, *Works and Days* (90). "Before what was released from the jar, mankind had no need of toilsome labor, there were no sickness and evils in life."

She asks, *Is it because I'm not Jewish?*

Scholars holding this view (e.g., Walcot 1961, 250) point out that the jar is termed an "unbreakable" (in Greek: *arrektos*) house. In Homer, and elsewhere in Hesiod, *arrektos* is applied to a structure meant to sequester its contents.

She asks, *Why not, if Rahel and Tehila let me in?*

Cf. Verdenius (65). "It was not her cunning… that prompted her to open the jar, but her curiosity."

She asks, *Why don't you know?*

Cf. Hesiod: "Only hope remained there, in an unbreakable home within, under the rim of the great jar."

She says, *Will she still let me turn out the lights on the Sabbath?*

Like the Serpent in Eden Is the Trumpet Vine

Of its creeping signs, I need to inform my new neighbor.
When we first arrived, some years before, a lovely cluster

hung like hair over the back deck, the blood-orange trumpets
trumpeting the sound of blood-orange. For seasons, while we slept,

it grew as our children grew, unnoticed, leaping slow-motion
from lattice to apple tree a body's length away, near the chain

link, anchoring its tendrils, until, between deck and apple,
it made a tent of shade. Then the apple died, strangled

by mute trumpets. The lattice tore, muscled out by vine's desire.
Even the throttled evergreen turned brown. Last summer,

I dug five tentacles, poured boiling water on roots,
razing it from root to shoot. Thought I'd won. This spring, it threw

ten hands through the deck, and farther, to the neighbor's tree,
the frantic flinging of a creature not yet ready

to die. I tell my neighbor, *Watch this vine. It will invade
the yard, crack the foundation.* Jonathan yawns, exhausted

father of four, not enough time to wrestle with gardens.
I say, *It's wound around the link. You'll have to cut the fence...*

What do you do? I ask. I study Torah. *Rabbinical
track?* I ask. Maybe. Studying Torah doesn't pay well.

The world doesn't pay well for the spirit, I say. Smiling,
he shakes his head, weary. Beneath the surface of the seen,

as rain turns to snow, the vines coil and ache and wait for spring.
Keep your eyes open, I say. I will, he says. We

pause to consider the intricate trouble of beauty.

Quarta Asia tabula continet Cyprum and Syrium and Iudea and Utraq.
Arabia petream and deserta ac Mesopotamia and Babilonia
[1541, edited by Michael Servetus]

Regarding Ptolemy's *Geographia,* Servetus's annotations brought him into conflict with Calvin, contradicting the biblical vision of a Land of Milk and Honey:

> "You must know, reader, that so big goodness was attributed [to this land] by sheer boasting; since the experience of merchants and pilgrims shows that this land is uncultivated, sterile and lacks any sweetness (comfortability); for that reason call the promised land the awaited land, but do not praise it in your vernacular language."

> *Where are Rahel and Tehila moving?* My daughter asks, after a day playing.
> They're going to Israel.
> *Why?*

Some believe that Servetus's mother was a *conversa,* a Jew who endured forced conversion. He'd learned Hebrew and Arabic, fought doctrines separating the three faiths of the Book.

> *Why?*
> (How to translate expulsion, Inquisition, pogroms, Holocaust?
> And aliyah, the longing for Zion, the Jerusalem of Gold?)

Burning was the penalty for heresy. Calvin advocated that Servetus receive beheading, but the matter had passed beyond his control.

> I think they have family there.
> *I want them to stay.*
> Me too.

A large crowd had gathered
The last copy of his book

Chained to his leg

[   ]

I'm trying to return   I'm looking ahead

to the you I knew   to the place we are
knew the one I was   already an us

                        and the child was
                        a blessed knife carving

I want to see   We could not see
how we were   to see the aching

                        us from ourselves, us
                        from each other

in the ribbed   stone, the years
nave of before   of haul and hoist

                        and the years feasted
                        on the presence of absence

what is the exile   what is the beloved
but one whose dreams   but what you cannot take

                        the longing a harvesting
                        of seeds from sleep

weigh less than clouds   weighs more than earth
simplified by rain   multiplied by rain

to look ahead   to attempt return

Panel [board] concerning the country of Canaan, the natural Israel, Palestine,
and the Jewish holy land called: was aforetime the Paradyse, full of good fruit,
grain, wine, balsamic, oil, etc. But after the Emperors Vespasian, Titus, and
Hadrian burned, and roughened, and destroyed it, it is a barren, miserable
country, a oed wuest place, bit at the end of the world
[Adam Reissner, Franckfurt am Main, 1563]

I cut and paste the title of the German map into Google

      aforetime the Paradyse

trying to find its rightful name, as if called
by its rightful name, it might appear

                            Reissner's map is 228 × 320 mm

                            Or, to convert into inches: 9 × 12.6

      A oed wuest place?

In Reissner's map, Jerusalem is a topographic tabula rasa
onto which the Temple of Solomon, as written, hovers

                            A quest location?
                            A local question?

making way for a return

But what if translations mistake, convert, or erase

      A oed wuest place

[Family]

At the Catholic university, a speaker clicks through slide after slide
of barbed wire, cattle-chute checkpoints, and walls. His mantra:
occupation. What threatens the Christians, he concludes, is what
threatens Palestinians. A woman stands up. *I wanted to let everyone
know,* she says, *that this talk was FULL of SPIN.* (I can't see her, she's
behind me, I'm afraid to look back.) *The truth is the OPPOSITE.*
(My heart goes out to her, standing in the heart of another country.)
The reason for the wall was that people were being ATTACKED, she
says. *BY TERRORISTS. After all, the Arabs sold the land, it was too
much trouble.* (I shrink back in my seat.) *And at a Catholic school, you
should KNOW what the Church has done, especially during World War
II!* Then a man gets up (I can't see him, he's behind me, I'm afraid
to look back). *The Jews bought a tiny bit of land, but the rest, the rest
was STOLEN!* (My heart goes out to him, standing in the heart of
another country.) *BUT!* he says. *THEY did not buy everything, even if
they buy Congress!* (I shrink again.) She says, *YOU have FOURTEEN
ARAB countries! Can't we have just ONE? THEY should take you in.*
He says, *but this is OUR land! Why should we have to leave? Because
EUROPE took it from us? That is why we fight!* (*What about PEACE?*
someone mumbles.) He says, *how can you negotiate over a pizza when
one side continues to EAT!* She says, *how can you negotiate over a pizza
when one side is trying to STAB you with knives!* It goes on like this
for a long time. Years. Decades. Generations. I sit like a child at the
table, watch parents grip utensils, spit words like shrapnel. I hate

> how I love them.
> Ashamed, I look down, unable
> to bury the hot metal.

Gaza/Sderot

A description of the Holy Land, not because the places of the continent, of which mention is made from the four writers of the gospel, but there are some other places by the sea

During patrols inside the casbah, we had mappings to do. *We're breathing behind you.* We go into a house to see who lives there. *You never know where.* It's 3 a.m. *You never know when.* The commander makes a drawing, what it looks like inside. *You never know why.* He says: "stand them against the wall and take their pictures." *And thus we injure.* I'm a young soldier. I do as they say. I take them. *And thus we do not end.* I kept the pictures for days. No arrests made. *We're breathing inside your head.* No one came to get them. No commander asked for them. *You'll never know when.* When I look at their faces, their eyes look dead. *Inside your head.* What if I got past that look? Could I follow? *You'll never know.*

[   ]

you there between things

                                        and the words for things

for a taste of your mouth I forsake gorging
                        for giving this my body your body always but suddenly

between things and the words for things
                        for your shining eyes slide over my nighted sight

I want to dispel the delusion of separation
                                        almost enough to shatter the glass of self

forgive our body always but suddenly
                                there is this singing

this inexplicable turning as bird follows spring
                                its translucent skull tuned to gathering light

and though I tunnel mute this tongue
                                works a small space open

                                        with one wet wing

[   ]

In the sudden chill, dogwood leaves blush. I no longer jog shirtless along sidewalks of the Orthodox, stitched kippas and flowing wigs hugging the skull, shielding the immodesty of hair. The sound of hammering in the air, to nail temporary wooden homes outside less temporary homes, to remember how the ancestors wandered, their heads filled with words read from right to left, and left to right the ways the people had fallen away from the unnameable. Years ago, I canvassed for Kerry, talking at screen doors and shaking heads, promising his dogged support for Israel, knowing it could mean a wall between Ummi and olive trees she worries over like children. We saw each other on each side of a screen. I told the story to five shaking heads, then two bright nods to vote. I carried the light of those promises back home. I love the Sabbath, how my neighbors sojourn from home to God, and God to home, carrying their story as scrolls on shoulders, sheathed in plastic during rain. Today, I jog past the sukkahs wearing a *Shalom* and *Salaam* T-shirt, a flag above each lung, two languages, *peace* and *hello.* I pass confused faces translating my chest, a language my neighbors know and do not know.

Palestinae delineatio ad geographiae canones revocata

As there is no adequate Arabic version of "as the crow flies"

When you come into the land of Canaan
That is the land
That shall fall unto you

The Delineation of the Borders [1603]

We are the distance

The Holy Land once the Promised Land or Palestine

The distance

Of the journey in the wilderness and the conquest and partition

And as we were worthy of sketching it so will we be worthy, with our own eyes

The distance

As today it is called

Of seeing walls rise

The distance between birds and Jerusalem

Kafr Yar/Babi Qasim

all Yids of Kiev city must gather

        heading back to the village from the harvest

and bring your documents and valuables

        and some rode horse-drawn carts / others, bicycles

if they open fire with gloved revolvers

        if in Kafr Qasim they order / *reap them*

some may choose to circle and shield you from

        you circle to choose the one to shield from

you must not breathe / when kicked you must not move

        you must live the death they have come to prove

bear the boot on your cheek / dirt on your face

        and be the dead that they have come to make

remember the names of the ones who covered you

        whose riddled bodies your voice now speaks through

Palaestinae quatuor facies [1720]

    This country exists as the fulfillment of a promise made by God Himself, the
prime minister asserted.

Near the School of Theology's library entrance, inside a glass display:
a book of the history of the Christian Church, written in Latin,
donated by prominent alumni,

wrapped in unusual skin.

It wasn't my college, but it could have been.
Our college was bought by the sale of Africans.

    It would be ridiculous to ask it to account for its legitimacy, the prime minister said.

    How can we return

            at night, love, your dark body is

                  Ayn Hawd became Ein Hod
              Nahlal arose in the place of Mahlul
               Ashdod in the place of Isdoud
                    Jaffa became Yafo

    the occupied territories? There is nobody

            hidden by hundreds of eyes of light

    to return them to.

The book was wrapped in the skin of a Native American.

[   ]

I don't know / you
don't know and want

your mouth open
to my mouth open

                                        what will it look
                                        look like I want

on to the names
and not let go

You manhandle my hand, draw it
across the bedded dark to cradle
your unfettered breast, and in the blind
hour rouse me to your body's fire

When I'm half-dream, and you're
half-dream, this skin is a borderland
without names and laws,
and everything rhymes with everything

                                        want to get lost
                                        lost in these maps

on to the names
and not let go

                                naming places
                                places not seen

but endlessly
imagined hold

[The Daily Contortions]

He's rushing down the block, away from shul, dressed in black hat, black coat and pants, black socks peeking beneath lemon-yellow Crocs. *Yom Kippur*—my daughter's eight-year-old friend Rahel informs us—*you can't wear leather, you don't eat, you get the chance to become an angel.* The kids are gathered around Yael's swing, whose arc's so wide you wonder if you're flying. The only grown-up, I give *underdogs*, which means helping others to *wing*, as Leila says, still lacking letters. Yael, our neighbor, the spit and image of my daughter, refuses her pretzels: *I don't give non-Jews pretzels*, she explains, then, *but I can give them to my dog. But Adele's almost Jewish*, Rahel insists. *Aren't you, Adele?* Who among us does not want *pretiola*—"little rewards" that monks would grant to children reciting Bible verses, which, read wrongly, one day would darken into Kristallnacht? The little arms folded in prayer, a crucifixion treat to savor and swallow. Here, the daily contortions continue. Who can do what and who cannot and by what law is it possible, and to sate which God hungry for our obedience? I want to shake this little angel, her flaming words expelling my daughter from the garden of her sunburned yard. I don't know what to say. But like in the dream, when a door opens to another room in your home, Rahel turns and breaks her pretzel, handing the savory splinter to Adele.

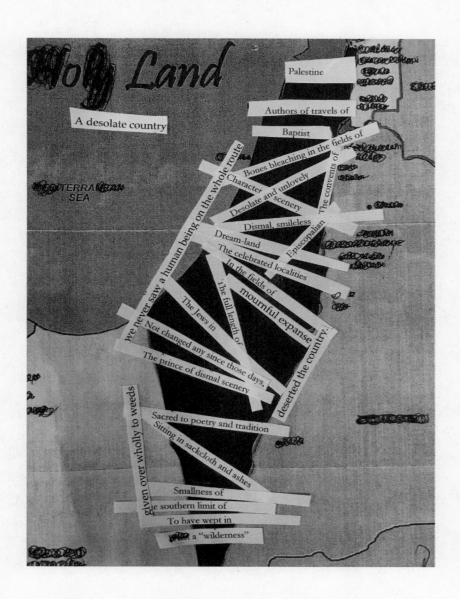

VII

Demolition Diptych

for Ezra Nawi

1.

look how they live / how easy to kick in the corrugate
and enter rifle-first / adjust the helmet in the unlit

interior / this sweat-heavy stable / no resistance just
these bleating sheep that speak / and we steer the trouble

-making cameraman and these people with rifles
out / the door we made / in the wall / no one

was shot / everyone's breathing / the laughing dozer
completes the deed / adrenaline flares its burning

currents through / our neural circuits and muscles still
twitching in delight / as after a night of drunk and black

out against dusty truck we lean and suck the starry
nicotine into flared lungs / and tonight when we return

to our own beds alive / alive unable / to sleep unable to
dream we will see everything fold again / like a house

2.

for Ezra would dive beneath the half-
demolished shell of a house / as if to stave off

what has already happened / ghost of where and what
he is / Jew and Arab / standing among Arabs who can't

understand why their house must fall
and why the bulldozer's teeth must sink into its chest

a lung collapsing / on the video you hear
Ezra's adrenaline gasping / in trembling hands

the soldier binds in plastic cuffs tighter and then
tighter again / "why are you tightening them?"

the soldiers laugh / "is it funny, the kids will sleep outside?"
and "the only thing left here is hatred"

"I did what my heart told me to do" / and "I will lodge
an immediate appeal" / for *Ezra* in Hebrew means "help"

Marginalia with Uprooted Olive

for Emad Burnat

the margin is
not the margin

to the margin /
above, the drone

trails a sound
like a mower

cutting the sky /
you look up

precedence for seizure
stand with

fellahin and land
in prison / in the

margin to turn
outside is to

riddle the inside
congratulation din

you stake your right
stalk and scrawl

across the white lawn
of law / they write

you gone / old weed
you will

not leave your
stony margin your

roots like limbs
claim horizon

VIII.
Returning to Jaffa

for Nahida Halaby Gordon

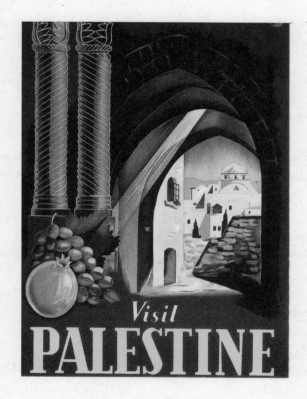

I couldn't understand. Why did the inhabitants [of Jaffa]... leave?

David Ben-Gurion

May 18, 1948

Bride of Palestine: to be read by four people simultaneously

Guidebook

Welcome to Jaffa!
Welcome to arched alleys
Bathing in sun

Welcome to this hive of new
Galleries and studios
Bars and clubs

Some say Jaffa was named
After Noah's son Japheth

Others that the Canaanites
Named it Yafi: beautiful

Welcome to chic
Minimalism with flea-
Market inspired accessories

First the Egyptians, then
Phoenicians, Babylonians,
Philistines, Assyrians,
Maccabees, Seleucids,
Persians, Greeks, Romans,
Crusaders, Mongols, Mamluks,
Ottomans, French, British, and
Zionist militias: now you!

Where Jonah embarked
Before the whale,

Welcome to Jaffa!

Haganah Leaflet

I hereby direct as follows:

All males will concentrate be-
tween Feisal Street, Al Mukhtar
Street, Al Hulwa Street and the
Sea

the particulars of which will be
notified later.

Outside those enclosures, normal
life for all peaceful Arabs may
continue

All persons will be issued with
a special identity-card and will
be free to return to their former
homes

All public Offices, Municipal
and Government, must be kept
intact and all documents and
registers therein must be kept
safely in good condition so that
any claims of residents may be
checked.

Yafa/Joppa/Jaffa/Yafo

Bride of Palestine

City of Oranges

From sunset until dawn
they did not spare
any house from shooting
We had no one
outside to help us

The mortar barrage designed to
cause chaos among the civilian
population to cause chaos in order
to create mass flight

chaos in order

houses dynamited
people still in them

unknown number

drowned during the exodus by sea

Nahida

Back then we lived as though
the Bible happened yesterday.
I'd fall asleep to the lighthouse
sweeping across our windows, a
comfort from explosions.

I saw a man carrying a coffin lid
like a shield, the shuffle of their
feet the only sound.

In the coffin, a clean-shaven
man in charcoal-gray suit, as if
dressed for a wedding.

"If you do not want the same
thing to happen to you as hap-
pened in Deir Yassin," we heard
the loudspeakers say, "then you
will flee."

Our bags packed, we drove
past houses in flames houses in
houses in houses in flames

Without those documents I
could never prove I lived there
that this house was mine this
life was mine

2. Reading of Tel Aviv and Jaffa, Flying Eastward

The airtight interior
        wags in the turbulence as I flip through
a glossy mag, trying to forget
        my body's longing to fall, farther, faster

than leaflets hauled from a hull
        declaring all young men must gather,
Jaffa, May 1948.
        Nahida's father would stash the flyer

she now resurrects for each
        PowerPoint presentation in Cleveland, half
a century away. "Three Days
        in Tel Aviv," the headline reads, where in "Yafo"

you can "haggle the gruff
        proprietor" of the local "junk shop,"
full of "ancient" castoffs,
        or partake of the bubbling narghile pipe.

The jet stream shimmies
        the jet, quaking ice in the plastic cup.
O Tel Aviv, "The Bubble"
        in which we live and don't live. O White City.

"Sometimes we feel like
        we're in the mouth," one artist laments,
"of a volcano. Sometimes
        we just want to drink and dance."

The Israeli artist wants
         to translate everything that's written
on Jaffa's Arab walls
         from the native tongue into a language

"tourists can understand." Today,
         a new post from Nahida, the attached
photos housing the only
         version of her home she will ever

get back. The plane
         jumps in a river of turbulence, the one
we'll leap in once,
         as unnamed flyover cities burn

their lights so far below it seems one breath
         could blow them out.

3. Postcard, "Tel Aviv (Explore Old Jaffa)"

4. The Palestinian Refugee's PowerPoint

But she doesn't look like a refugee, my student said, eyeing
her grandmotherly cardigan, her gray-black coif and new laptop.

I've asked her to tell *her* story, but on her PowerPoint,
It is 1948. I am nine. I'll tell you only what I know

she's mired in last century, laserpointing Balfour and Rothschild, Sykes and Picot,
I know: a pain behind my ribs when I cast back

the diminishing green of Palestine on map after digital map
into the river of remember. Tremor of explosion

as if, clicking past resolutions and broken accords, trying to piece together
near the town center, January 4, and my father there, and now

a shrapneled map, a forensic scientist examining her own body, trying to explain
in the bathroom, his black hair ash-white, my mother combing out the stones,

and gathering her strength to touch the hurting place,
her hand quaking, his blue suit chalk-white, his silk tie

and my sophomores, soporific from history, slip into a dream
soaked red, and I'm asking why, why,

or glance at their screens, seeing or not seeing
years later, his hand still holding the last Haganah leaflet

what it takes her to return

fallen from the sky.

INSTRUCTIONS TO THE ARAB POPULATION

by the

COMMANDER of the Hagena,

Tel-Aviv District

Given on

13th May 1948.

WHEREAS your representatives signed an Agreement today, I hereby direct as follows :

1.　　　Any shot fired at a Jewish area or at a Jew or at any member of the Hagana, or any resistance to them, will be sufficient reason for the Hagana to open fire at the Offender.

2.　　　All arms, ammunition and military equipment of any kind will be stacked at a place and time which will be notified later, and handed over to my representative. Any person found in possession of any article of military equipment after that time will be severely punished.

3.　　　Any person having any knowledge or information of the location of mines or booby traps or any similar devices, will at once submit such information to the nearest member of representative of the Hagana. Any person disobeying this order will be severely punished.

4.　　　(a) All males in the area defined in the Agreement will concentrate in the area between Feisal Street, Al Mukhtar Street, Al Hulwa Street and the Sea until everybody has identified himself under arrangements, the particulars of which will be notified later.

　　　(b) During this time, any male found outside this area will be severely punished, unless in possession of a special permit

5.　　　After the termination of the identification, all persons with the exception of those defined in Paragraph 6 will be issued with a special identity-card and will be free to return to their former homes unless they live in an area which will be declared as a military enclosure.

6.　　　All persons who may be dangerous to the peace and security of the area will be interrogated and, if necessary, be interned. The Representatives of the Arab population may attend in an advisory capacity during these proceedings.

　　　The Commander of the Hagana declares that it is not his intention to detain and/ or to intern the male population of the area defined, even if they or any of them did take part in the hostilities in the past. Only criminals or persons suspected of being a danger to the peace are liable to internment.

7.   The number and the size of the military enclosures, i.e. areas out of bounds to civilians, will be limited and directed by military necessities only. Outside those enclosures, normal life for all peaceful Arabs may continue in the whole area.

8.   Any male wishing to leave may apply to my representative for a permit to do so; likewise any male Arab who left Jaffa and who wishes to return to Jaffa may apply for a permit to do so. Permits will be granted after their bonda-fides have been proved, provided that the Commander of the Haganais convinced that applicants will not, at any time, constitute a threat to peace and security. This will be done with the cooperation of the representatives of the Arab population, who will funtion in an advisory capacity.

9.   All public Offices, Municipal and Government, must be kept intact and all documents and registers therein must be kept safely in good condition so that any claims of residents may be checked.

10.   The removal or transfer of any property within the area defined must be previously authorised by my representative.

11.   The ensure that these and any further instructions will be carried out, I shall nominate a representative who will help restore law and order in Jaffa.

12.   Public Health and other Public Utility Services of the Municipality of Tel-Aviv will endeavour to assist you until normal life is established in Jaffa.

6. Passages Marked

Two holes ghost the top of the page, as if punched for a legal file.
                    Someone pounded out the agreement on a manual. Evidence:

Stiff keys. Every letter partially inked.
                    Someone's fingers tapping

Any person as *Amy person.*
                              Back then we lived in the land of the Bible as though it happened yesterday
                                      Simon the Tanner's shop a short walk from our house

The page creased into three
                              because of the stench, tanning was considered unclean, but Peter stayed

"…who wishes to return to Jaffa may apply…"

                    as if opened and read and showed to others
                                      not afraid of taking a meal from one considered an outcast

"…after their bonda-fides have been proved…"

                    certain passages marked with pink pen
                              and later, when Peter visited a Roman centurion, the Spirit of the Lord

"…must be kept safely in good condition…"

                    and folded again, many times, carried carefully across borders
                              descended, that no one could stand in the way of anyone baptized with water

                    and opened again

7. Return (I)

First, it was a restaurant. Next door, a woman sat smoking.

Did she feel guilty about living in someone else's home?

"No. I have had a hard life and I deserve this apartment. I was born on a kibbutz, and life was hard there."

8. A Tour of Deir Yassin as Broken Ghazal

Activists carried the names of 100   in Deir Yassin.

> *Prior to the massacre, we were on good terms with the Jews in Givat Shaul. We shared food, celebrated together, paid condolences to one another, babysat for each other [in Deir Yassin].*

The majority of the   women, children or elderly despite   time
                        were   in Deir Yassin

> *My grandmother's cousin, Naziha Radwan, was six   . She survived by covering in her grandmother's blood, hiding beneath stiffened and pretending to be*

            the remnants of   cemetery,   bulldozed in the   0s.
Two days before   "Death to Arabs" painted on
                                            in Deir Yassin

> *Tell the soldiers: you have made history in Israel with your attack and your conquest. . . .*
>
>   *As in Deir Yassin,*

> *so everywhere, we will attack and smite the enemy. God, Thou has chosen us for conquest.*

An elderly man joined the tour and described   Yair Zaban had been
                                in Deir Yassin

the day after, removing Palestinian   ,
> *the most difficult thing [I] had done in [my] life.* Deir Yassin

        is now

            shopping centers, bus depots, religious Jewish schools, a psychiatric hospital
            of Givat Shaul Bet and

9. The Particulars of Which

                nights I'd fall asleep to the lighthouse sweeping its beam across our windows

Diso beying

                                     a constant comfort

a space in the middle

                                     from the explosions

of the word, typed hastily

o beying

                I have no memories of walking streets of Yafa just the scenes from our balcony

"All males… will concentrate… between Feisal Street, Al Mukhtar Street, Al Hulwa Street…"
                              a man carrying a coffin lid like a shield

"…and the Sea until everybody has identified…"
                           the shuffle of their feet the only sound

"…identified himself under arrangements…"
                           in the coffin, a clean-shaven man in

the Irgun's steady rain of mortar fire
                           charcoal-gray suit, as if

          O City of Oranges, O Bride of Palestine
                          dressed for a wedding

"…the particulars of which will be…"

        "if you do not want the same thing to happen to you as happened in Deir Yassin,"
                 we heard the loudspeakers say, "then you will flee"
                 our bags packed, we drove past houses in flames

How many thousands were pushed out behind barbed wire drowned at sea

houses in flames

"…the particulars of which will be…"

declared absentees

"…notified later…"

O Bride

"…free to return to their former homes…"

taken by the State

never to return or be returned

10. Begin + *Uprooting* by Tamam Al-Akhal

Soldiers of the Irgun! We are going to conquer Jaffa. This will be one of the most decisive battles in the war for Israel's independence. Know who is before you, remember those you have left behind. You face a ruthless enemy, who intends to wipe us out. Behind you are your parents, our brothers and our children. Snipe the enemy. Aim well, conserve ammunition.

Show no mercy in battle, just as the enemy has no pity for our people. Be compassionate to the women and children. Whoever lifts his hand in surrender, spare him.

11. Ode to the Oranges of Jaffa

> *My father used to buy the ones too large to ship. We'd scoop the insides and eat it*
> *and then make jack-o'-lanterns out of them.*
>
> Nahida Halaby Gordon

For you're oval and thick-peeled, easy
to remove. For you're seedless and tough

skinned and suitable for export.
For your juice starts sweet, then runs

bitter. For *naranj* comes from Sanskrit,
meaning "fruit like elephants." Memory

the earth you come from, and perfume
the whole city, when wind pages through

your leaves. For by 1845, thirty-eight million
shipped to farther shores. Then symbol

of Arab-Jewish cooperation, before the war,
then orange engine of the new Israel.

For the last Jew to grow them now says, *to cut*
the orchard down would be to cut out my heart.

12. Postcard, "Summon the Genie of the Jaffa to guard your health!"

13. Return (II)

Then, years later, it was an apartment complex. When my father remodeled the property before the war, he built a secret chamber within the steps, placing several bottles of wine that he planned to serve at his children's weddings. The steps were now gone.

14. The House on Ajami

15. Return (III)

And then it was a shop, more apartments. The shop was "The Israeli Experience." I asked the owner, "what about the 'Palestinian Experience'?" He became enraged, told me I knew nothing. One occupant allowed us into her home. We sat and reminisced about the house as though it were a common acquaintance. She thought the Church had owned it. We talked politics, rising fascism, her family's escape from pogroms. I felt her suffering. In a different time, we could have been friends. When I got up to leave, I hugged her, and she returned my hug.

16. About the Municipal Historical Archives

(http://tel-aviv.millenium.org.il/The+Municipal+Historical+Archives.htm)

The Municipal Archives are the historical archives of the Municipality of Tel Aviv–Yafo from the founding of the "Achuzat Bayit" Association in 1906 until about 1990.

The collections of the archives reflect the history of the city in all the fields in which municipality is involved: matters of education and culture, construction, gardens, religion etc. The municipal archives also contains private papers, like the Chamber of Commerce, the Commercial Club and of private people. The collections include also maps beginning from the twenties, historical photographs, publications of the municipality and posters.

The archives is the center of information of the history of the city and is opened to all. Workers of the archives will answer, with pleasure, questions about the collections of the archives and will provide historical information, if its location does not require lengthy search.

There are also few previous papers of the Jewish Community of Jaffa (Vaad Hakehilla) of the years 1896–1898. Unfortunately, the majority of the archives of the Municipality of Jaffa prior to 1948 have been lost

17. Tabitha, Arise

"Outside those enclosures, normal life"

In Yafa I attended Tabeetha School for Girls
named after the girl brought back from death

Now there was at Joppa a certain disciple named Tabitha
full of good works and almsdeeds

A pink pen mark along the left margin highlights passages:

"All public Offices… must be kept intact and all documents and registers therein…"

we escaped by car in April 1948 shortly after Yafa fell
the houses in flames

And it came to pass in those days, that she was sick, and died

"…must be kept safely in good condition…"

without those documents
I could never prove that I lived there
that this house was mine
this life was mine

Then Peter went with them and all the widows stood by weeping

"…so that any claims of residents may be…"

And prayed; and turning to the body he said, Tabitha, arise

the registrar of the Tabeetha School had saved a few registers
when she heard I was looking
she had not forgotten

"…will endeavor to assist you…"

And she opened her eyes, and when she saw Peter, she sat up

sixty years later she showed me the book, and opened it
I could see my name:

"…so that any claims of residents may be…"

and I could see my name
my name, alongside my classmates' names

"…until normal life…"

(I held it in my palms)
I existed still
to see my name, carefully written

in someone's hand

"…will endeavor to assist you…"

And it was known throughout all Joppa

Nahida Halaby

18. Register

Consecutive Admission Number	Readmission Original Number	Date of Admission or Readmission			PUPIL'S NAME	Birth			
		D	M	Y		D	M	Y	
						9	6	40	G
201					Bordcosh Laila	23	6	40	
202					Halaby Donees	10	6	40	
203					Attallah Mimi	19	9	39	
204					Halaby Nahida	16	1	40	
205					Saroof Diana	16	1	40	G
206					Nassoura Widad	28	3	40	
207					Farooki Reima	13	9	40	G
208					Kutteh Nabil	13	3	40	
209					Sabbagha George	28	3	40	
210					Abou Khadra Nabil	20	5	40	
211					Halaby Rurik	3	2	40	
212					Abou Geben Nadim	4	6	39	
213					Kayaleh Abed	26	5	40	
214					Bernstein Steven	10	10	38	
215					Azzi Amal	18	3	42	G
216					Bordcosh Reima	19	6	40	
217					Kattan Randa	19	3	41	
218					Hindeleh Reitsa	26	8	39	
219					Sifri Charlotte	30	5	42	
220					Andraus Suad	1	10	41	
221					Khalaf Hanna	1	9	40	
222					Haieiri Tahida	16	3	40	
223					Bishara Souhaila	9	9	40	
224					Rodenko Olla	19	6	41	
225					Tamari Taina	9	11	42	
226					Qudweh Maha	9	10	40	
227					Taji Taher				

andi	Father	Abedel Raoof St.	
hadeh		Ajami Str	
aad	"	Ajami	
odol	"	Saroof Adv. Service	
hara	"	Abedel Raoof St.	
bour		Jabaliah	
as		Ajami	
usbak	"	Abow Jibain St	
ndali	"	Ajami St	
eed		Hilweh St.	
del	"	Ajami St.	
andi	Father	Ajami St.	
yeeb	Father	Box 263	
afac	"	Ajami	
rahim	"	Faisal St.	
nin	"	Jabalieh	
ad Deen	"	P.O.B. 503	
mi		Jabaliah	
orge		Nuzha Str.	
aig		Ajami Street	
bed	Father	P.O.B 452	
id Deen		P.O.B 503	

IX.

When It Rains in Gaza

for Deema Shehabi

I.

I tap my cell to see
a dark-haired girl, flute-armed:

Amal salvaging history
texts from yesterday's

ancient ruins. Her home.
The walls around me

are stable. Amid rubble
she rises in a green hoodie,

gripping a bent spine
of a book, its pages furling

dust. I'm not there or here
when she presses the book

to her chest, pauses to eye us,
then disappears inside the pages.

2.

Inside her book
is a tunnel dug at night—

not one, but dozens of them
beneath the rubble

beneath surveillance
drones churning above—

hundreds yawning in the dark,
dug by shovel and hunger,

as if people were rodents
no walls could hinder:

computers and donkeys,
brides and coils of rebar, small

arms, rockets, flour—white
blood cells of the stateless.

3.

And inside this bomb
is Rahed Taysir al-Hom.

Twenty years—with pliers
and screwdrivers, wire

cutters and silence
and patience and no body

armor—he dismantled
death, patiently defused

stray missiles, rockets, land
mines. He refused

no one. *Very brave,*
but slow, one man complained,

the bomb in our home
waiting for weeks. Until today.

4.
When it rains in Gaza, the tin roofs clatter
so loud even the teacher can't be heard.

5.
Of fragment of metal,
propelled by farm

fertilizer and melted sugar.
Inside the slurry is anger,

analysis of angles and wind
resistance, deprivation

raised to a prayer.
Of the seventy mosques

and seven thousand homes
welcomed to oblivion,

which saw rockets designed
to return where ancestors lived,

a land they have dreamed
to touch with their feet?

6. AL-AWDA MEANS RETURN

What the al-Awda ice-cream factory
(this is not news, this is not poetry)

in addition to storing medicine
may or may not have been hiding, since

the factory was bombed, we cannot know.
The owner says, *I live inside. I go*

to sleep listening to production lines.
No rockets made in here, just butter. Why?

It smells of burning plastic and butter.
How would it taste, the sweetness of return?

Because there was no room in morgues, babies
curled in ice-cream freezers. And every day,

the sea churned a white froth, salting the air,
lapping the sand as if there were no war.

7.

Above the tub, Salem Saoody leans,
grinning and palming the frothing water

over niece and daughter, their hair slicked
with soap, their bodies gleaming in the brisk

delight of being bubble-wet and clean. Pull
back. Around the tub, the ceiling in piles—

the walls just a few columns and open.
The whole neighborhood a roofless ruin,

a movie set for apocalypse. After.
Welcome to the desert of the real.

Just the tub survives this Operation
Protective Edge. So focus in: laughter

and water, froth and a father's smile.
The heart will break what the eye can't swallow.

8.

When it rains in Gaza, children run out
of noise, lift their open lips to heaven.

9. WHITE PHOSPHORUS

A jellyfish of smoke,
you say aloud, *Look!*—

the beautiful photo's
white tentacles and head

swim the sky
before they fall. A privacy

of glass. Ripples
of division. Flesh

from flesh, true god
from true god, made

in the walled
island of unforgiven

not unforgotten, dreaming
where the past will lead.

10. DRONE

A sky's eye, tracking
by heat of body,

a hive-mind locking
in its tar-

get. The dark
is white. The heat

of flesh is dark. Arms
rise—planting

white explosives,
or clipping black

linens to a black
line to dry

beneath a black
unmovable sun?

11.

Operation Summer Rains tomorrow,
followed by Operation Autumn Clouds.

You can read all the statistics online.
The heroic couplet cosigns to a lie.

Operation Cast Lead will hit the coast,
then Operation Pillar of Defense.

Write: Israel-Palestine? Palestine-
Israel? Hyphens bridge, burn, or blind.

And then Operation Protective Edge.
Cease-fire. The advancing age of siege.

12.

Over the wall, other people stroll
the tree-green streets of Sderot.

Deep inside each mind, a missile itches
a place that only a missile can scratch.

Green is not just the color of Hamas,
but it is the color of Hamas. Hamas:

acronym for the Islamic Resistance,
Arabic for zeal, Hebrew for violence.

Did they know when they chose
their name? *Hamas* also means to seize.

13.

Deema, I want to soften the gnaw
of loss, break its teeth and plant them
in gardens, watch them grow

anchors in exile, your words
in my mouth migrating
back to you in California hills,

blooming with irises
and wildfire—but what do I know
of the migrant earth, as you

wrote, of entering a rooftop
in Gaza, watching your mother
widen into herself again, at home,

then having to part with your mother
again, at the country of skin?

14.

The forecast for Gaza today: Pleasant.
Beautiful. A row of icons of sun.

15.

Amal, I pray you
have not folded

inside phosphorus,
or nestled beside

uneaten ice cream.
There is no us.

There is no them.
That by late light

this night, you read
until you believe

the wall will fall
the siege will end

and missing walls
will rise again.

X.

Future Anterior

after Jeff Halper, David Shutkin, Eyal Weizman,
and Fazal Sheikh

1. *What is a settlement?*

Here's another olive tree.
As the walls rise, these trees,

which have been in families
for centuries, are taken,

uprooted, then replanted
in settlements, in fashion

among the nouveau riche.
Here is a shopping center:

Ace Hardware, Burger Ranch.
Another ancient olive tree.

This is the Library of Peace.
This is the music conservatory.

Look at the water
flowing from this fountain.

2. *What is a ruin?*

They said it was a ruin so they expelled the families who lived there, mostly in the caves. Who's to say what's a ruin, and what's a home? On the day of a prominent Bar Mitzvah, which occupied the new members of the town, the Center for Jewish Nonviolence bought tickets for the families expelled from Susiya, hundreds of people and their children. They toured their town, entering the mosque (now a synagogue), and we brought chairs and tables and had a big feast together. When everyone was full, and tired, they slowly climbed back onto the buses and left. I was the last one, cleaning up. Suddenly, an IDF bus pulled up, and soldiers came streaming out, all at the ready. But everyone was gone except me. A man with a JNF nameplate came up, put his arm around my shoulder, and said, "you win this round."

3. *What's the opposite of guarded?*

But where did the people go? Where do they go now?

4. *What is a ruin?*

when Issa was sentenced and buried
in parentheses / and his mother saw her house

slowly becoming debris / she slid
into a comma / she was driven

by ambulance / dashes to ashes /
pupils to colons / the new revised standard

replacing the old revised standard
replacing the King's version and so on

outside the house not-yet not-house
a nightingale offered quotation marks

around the bulldozer's boring
exclamations of / instant ancient ruins

footnote to a lengthy dissertation
on subject-object relations

5. *What's the opposite of ruin?*

Between the border of land and sea, the waves crest and purl, knitting and unknit-
ting the shore.

6. *What knows no border?*

Each year, half a billion birds fly across this land, this country of migration.

7. *What knows no walls?*

Eighty-five percent of West Bank water is funneled into the settlements or into
Israel. That's why you always see water tanks on Palestinian roofs. To say nothing
about Gaza.

8. *What knows no walls?*

The lower the bullet hole in the water tank,
the less the family can drink.

9. *What is a settlement again?*

"When the Lord your God brings you into the land he swore to your fathers, to Abraham, Isaac and Jacob, to give you—a land with large, flourishing cities you did not build, houses filled with all kinds of good things you did not provide, wells you did not dig, and vineyards and olive groves you did not plant—then when you eat and are satisfied, be careful that you do not forget the Lord, who brought you out of Egypt, out of the land of slavery."

10. *What is a settlement again?*

Before the wall, the village
sidled up to the wadi, as if in love

with the wadi, people streaming
from dream into olive leaves, rising

before the light, before the bulldozers,
before the red-roofed buildings rose

atop the neighboring hill, before
the hill grew barbed-wire perimeters,

before the cell tower lifted itself, before
the trailers encircled to protect it,

before there was a man driving the road
who lost his signal, and reported it

to the cell phone provider, who,
to comply with the law and serve

the customers, to ensure consistent
service, thus fulfilling the divine plan

of total cellular connectivity, before
the nations that come and go like seasons,

there was an olive sapling pulling itself
by its own internal music, composed

of breakable earth, occasional rains,
the rhythmic shifts of dark and light.

11. *What is the origin of "map"?*

Carta is Latin for paper.

Everything written
will have been
a map of the future anterior.

12. *What do people share?*

At midday in summer, the sun hammers you flat as tin.
You look for any shadow to hide in.

13. *What do you want others to know?*

Tell them that we exist.

                    That we exist,

even between the words of their text.

14. *What knows no state, no nation?*

From a certain height, in a certain light,
stretching across a plain

the land resembles warm skin

If you live long enough,

you can almost see it

breathing

My Heart like a Nation

for Yehuda Amichai

You threw off your exile
by clothing yourself in praise,
Yehuda, saying, *my nation
is alive,* Amichai, *in me,*

inhabiting your own body,
your mother-beloved skin.
I'm hairy like you, and afraid,
like you, I'm half animal

and half angel, uncertain
where my tenderness ends
and cruelty begins. *We
did what we had to do,*

you wrote, which in translation
reads: ███████████████
Yehuda, I want your clarity—
to love you, not close the gates

of my heart like a nation
trying to make itself a home
but winding up with a state.
Psalmist, you spoke so tenderly

of peace, but the war persists.
All I have for you is this poem:
a man photographs the sudden
undulating hills. Behind him,

a woman he loves now dreams
that their bed's legs grow roots
beneath, overnight, and spread
a canopy of branches that shoot

pink blooms open and open,
now green with shushing leaves
that shelter and shadow the rucked
bedsheets, the branches burdened

with red apples, apples like eyes
ready to be praised
                    and plucked.

Marginalia

Of this place I choose the wind.
Mahmoud Darwish

Your throne was
margin. Your voice

a ruin of Birwe,
the thrown

and the road.
What remains

of what you
walked on?

Of this place
you chose

the wind. Of
and of. Odysseus

and Scheherazade,
you woke

to morning inside
a suitcase. Yourself

and not yourself,
you are,

at last,
arced textures

housed in
our mouths.

You opened
the window,

all these rain
shards

our words.
You nearly

mastered
absence.

How dare
you die.

Script/A Paleography for the Future

for Michal Rovner

we are written
        we are writhing
                living letters
        in liquid text

we are bowing
        we are rowing
                over water
        ant-black silent

film / still and yet
        fulfill some script
                each our bodies
        syncing syntax

each pull threatens
        what has threaded us
                into this crowd
        is there meaning

in the moaning
        we can quite hear
                ought we quiet
        breathing labor

ought we coax her
        is it death pangs
                is it birth throes
        she is rowing

over darkness
    she is writing
        living letters
    in a liquid next

Isdoud

for Fady Joudah

dear descendant
of the dis
appeared you ascend

the pillar
of your own air
spin and span

whole abysses
with lines
translating there

to here and here
to where
wind winds

in dry wadis
hoists sea
in handful

after invisible
handful
isdoud now

your e-mail address
and digital image
of branches

through windows
within school ruins
a refugee points

with his cane
to what he
only can see

you argue against
the argument
against your

self you
yourself make
and home in

kiss my blind
eyes clear
close keyholes

with opening
homeland you
cradle in vowels

what was not
never yours
I'll hold it here

till you return

The Bullet Dream

for Majed Abbadi

In America, he lugs a thin shadow along his hip. In Palestine, years before, he'd been crossing the street, leaving his house, slipping through youth slinging stones, arced arias against their plight. The soldiers down the road, playing their part in this daily opera, unleashed a pack of bullets. The bite in his side. Dragged himself away, not to the hospital where blood was proof of guilt. A song lost inside a wall.

And when she, an American, fell for him he was so thin at first she could see it through his skin. When she moved in, it sank beneath flesh, but she could feel it with her hands, at night, when they turned soft to each other in bed. They moved to her country. One day, the old singing arose, the in him not him, pressing the other side of his skin. And when he walked out of the hospital, the leaden heaviness no longer troubled his hip, and when she asked to see it he said what.

Afterword

Shrapnel Maps is my journey to clarify the question of belonging in a land with so many different names that to try to speak them all is to become crowded with history: Canaan. The Land of Israel. אֶרֶץ יִשְׂרָאֵל. Palestine. فلسطين. The Holy Land. The Levant. The Middle East. The journey began at our family dinner table, questioning my sister in the late summer of 1993. She had just returned from Birzeit University near Ramallah, and burned with stories: settlers shooting at crowds, checkpoints, house demolitions, prison torture—a litany of atrocity, as if she'd been flung into an upside-down world behind a mirror. I wondered if she'd been brainwashed. It was the opposite of what I'd read in the newspapers. Her courage to stand in the truth of what she saw compelled me to look further. Subsequent friendships with Palestinians and Jews corroborated, complicated, and added texture to her stories.

My sister's path led our family to Palestine a decade later. "A Concordance of Leaves" details that 2003 visit to Toura in the West Bank for her wedding. My gratitude to Majed, his family, and the people of Toura for their generosity and kindness.

"Theater of Operations" is composed of monologue sonnets dramatizing a fictional suicide bombing. During the Second Intifada, 2000–2005, scores of suicide attacks wreaked terrible devastation, not only hundreds of Israeli lives lost but also the psychological trauma and distrust the attacks induced. At the same time, thousands of Palestinians also lost their lives resisting the occupation. "Theater" relies on language borrowed from news reports, comment threads, oral testimony, interviews, literature, and letters.

"Unto a Land I Will Show Thee" began as an inquiry into the history of mapping the land. While many of the poems are framed with the names of old maps, the setting is University Heights, Ohio, where we have lived for nearly two decades, home to a large Jewish Orthodox community and a Catholic college. As an Arab American, I've seen my experiences as a metaphor for navigating neighborliness in a divided society. In that sequence, I relied on borrowed text from a number of resources, especially the "Holy Land Maps" resource from the Eran Laor Cartographic Collection of the National Library of Israel. I employed language from *Holy Land in Maps* (Israel Museum, 2011), and have borrowed language from the Bible, an assignment in my daughter's Sunday school class, the poem "Landscape" by Fady Joudah, a lecture by Israeli ambassador Yoram Ettinger, a speech by Moshe Dayan, and Golda Meir.

"Returning to Jaffa" is dedicated to Nahida Halaby Gordon. Every year, Nahida comes to my course, Israeli and Palestinian Literatures, to share her personal testimony. Seventy years have not lessened the pain when she speaks of her final days in Jaffa, before her family—and other Palestinian families—fled in 1948. Nahida discovered the Haganah flyer in her father's papers after his death. It speaks to the level of planning in the military operation against Palestinians and against Jaffa's municipal records. This document needs to be included in the historical debate about responsibility for Palestinian refugees and the right of return. The fact that the flyer was written in English shows the British administration's presence in Palestine and forecasts how the new state would adopt some of its measures against unruly Palestine. Because of Jaffa's size—100,000 residents, 65,000 of whom were Palestinian—the UN Partition Plan (1947) actually designated the city as part of a future Palestinian state, but its geographical placement in the heart of the planned Israeli state made it particularly vulnerable. In a footnote to *City of Oranges: An Intimate History of Arabs and Jews in Jaffa* (W.W. Norton, 2007), Adam LeBor writes, "It is a curious footnote of the 1948 war in Jaffa that the municipal records until the end of the British Mandate no longer seem to exist. They are not at the Tel Aviv municipal archives.... Some Palestinians believe they were captured and either destroyed or locked away by the new Israeli authorities, to prevent any future claims over land ownership" (372). Israel deemed Palestinian properties "Absentee Properties," which were absorbed by the state, including Jaffa's orange groves that would fuel the Israeli economy during the lean years after the war. Please read Nahida's book *Palestine Is Our Home: Voices of Loss, Courage, and Steadfastness* (Palestine Books, 2016) to learn more stories of Palestinian refugees. The poems of "Returning to Jaffa" sometimes draw upon her words directly.

"When It Rains in Gaza" turns toward Gaza, particularly during Operation Protective Edge in 2014. I dedicate this poem to Deema K. Shehabi, and to the people of Gaza.

The "Visit" posters are the work of Mitchell Loeb, a Jewish American who ran a commercial art studio that produced the "Visit Palestine" posters for the Tourist Office of the Jewish Agency for Palestine in 1947, one year before Israel's independence and Palestine's Nakba. I have selectively cropped them, and in one case, "Weird Apparition," included an index of references to Arabs in Mark Twain's *The Innocents Abroad*.

The "Innocents Abroad" poems work with Twain's *The Innocents Abroad* (1869), a travelogue that depicts Palestine as a wasteland with a smattering of diseased humans—a massive erasure of local realities. I kept bumping into Twain's text online while researching Zionist narratives, which recycled his words as evidence that Palestine was a land without a people. The narratives lifted quotes directly from *From Time Immemorial: The Origins of the Arab-Jewish Conflict Over Palestine* (Harper & Row, 1984), a Zionist history that Norman Finkelstein has called a hoax text. The same quotes were again summoned—with the same ellipses that sometimes elided numerous pages—by another book, *A Durable Peace: Israel and Its Place among the Nations* (Warner Books, 1993, 2000), by Benjamin Netanyahu, the longtime Prime Minister of Israel.

In an interview, Palestinian poet Ghassan Zaqtan said:

> We have many civilizations in this place…. And if we accept that we are the conclusion of all of these histories, the narrative will be clearer. Some start history with the Battle of Ajnadayn, when the Muslims invaded Palestine 1,300 years ago, as if there is no history before that. This ignores 10,000 years. The Israelis start with the Hebrews' journey to Palestine. They ignore what happened after and they ignored what happened before…. It will never end that way. If you want to belong to this place, you have to belong to all of its history and respect 10,000 years of several civilizations.

Zaqtan calls us to a wider memory, and a wider sense of belonging, where no one is erased by another's dream of a place. Now living in Cuyahoga County, home of the crooked river that burned, I walk to work every day, wondering what's been erased—both far away, where my ancestors lived in the "Middle East," and close by, in this Midwest erased of Native Americans, and even closer, in my own heart and home. What countries could we see, and what countries could we make, if we erased the erasures?

As *Shrapnel Maps* began to move from the airy clouds of my head into the matter of text, I recalled Aaron Davidman saying that the conflict is not complicated like a car engine, but it is complex like a forest. Hearing him engage in passionate debate with my friends Debby and Glenn, I thought, if I can't sit inside the stories of Israelis and Palestinians, of Jews and Arabs, and open the gates of my heart to their exiles and returns, how could I ever expect those cut by the knives of history to do so?

I'm thinking again about my small window into life in that place of many names. The way the breeze, far from the sea in the West Bank, still carries the sea. The evanescent patterns of light through the leaves painting themselves on a white wall, built by patient and strong hands of the Abbadi family, with materials drawn out of the earth. Going to Umm ar-Rehan forest in the West Bank, surprised by the wild beauty of evergreen oak and Aleppo pine. How we couldn't leave the village, one day, because the IDF had bulldozed all the roads leading in, and so we drove across the rutted path between olive trees. How olive trees, everywhere, grow— never straight, but always toward the light and into themselves.

I'm thinking as well about my neighbor M—, a young rabbi with a big family, who occasionally needs a mitzvah during the holidays. Once, his son had turned on the gas stove and it started to burn a cupboard. Another time, the fridge light had turned on and he needed the censor taped back. I felt self-conscious as he watched me tape it, while around my wrist was a bracelet that read Free Palestine. I told my wife I was worried that he would be angry. She said, No, it's good. He needs to know that there are good people who also want freedom for Palestinians.

About the US, William Stafford once wrote: "We live in an occupied country, misunderstood; / justice will take us millions of intricate moves." We are here for such a short time, and then we are gone. I wonder: How can we listen better, attentive to the shards of pain, and invite the gentle flowing of kindness? What do we say to those who remain in the thickets of suffering? How can we dismantle the structures that destroy others and ourselves? What can we do in this brief space of our breathing? What will we make instead?

List of Illustrations

All illustrations and photographs by Philip Metres unless otherwise attributed

p.3 "Visit— ": Postcard by Mitchell Loeb (cropped)

p.8 Redaction of Mark Twain's *The Innocents Abroad*

p.9 "Remains" by Manal Deeb (cf. www.ygalleri.com)

p.39 "Visit Palestine/Weird Apparition" (original by Mitchell Loeb)

p.41 Redaction of Mark Twain's *The Innocents Abroad*

p.43 "Shattered Plates"

p.67 Redaction of Mark Twain's *The Innocents Abroad*

p.73 "Visit— ": Postcard by Mitchell Loeb

p.79 From *Hope & Healing in the Holy Land Lesson Plans* by The Holy Land
     Franciscans

p. 99 "O Land"

p.105 "Visit Palestine": Postcard by Mitchell Loeb (erasure)

p.110 "Tel Aviv (Explore Old Jaffa)": Postcard (artist unknown)

p.112–13 Haganah flyer courtesy of Nahida Halaby Gordon

p.119 "Uprooting" by Tamam Al-Akhal

p. 121 "Summon the Genie of the Jaffa to guard your health!": Postcard (unknown
     artist)

p.123 Photograph of "The House on Ajami" courtesy of Nahida Halaby Gordon

p.128–29 Register photograph courtesy of Nahida Halaby Gordon

p.131 "Visit— Mostcloud"

p.143 "Visit— Allcloud"

About the Author

Philip Metres is the author of ten books, including *Shrapnel Maps*, *The Sound of Listening: Poetry as Refuge and Resistance*, *Pictures at an Exhibition*, *Sand Opera*, and *I Burned at the Feast: Selected Poems of Arseny Tarkovsky*. His work has garnered fellowships from the Lannan Foundation and the National Endowment for the Arts, and he has received six Ohio Arts Council grants, the Hunt Prize, the Adrienne Rich Award, three Arab American Book Awards, the Watson Fellowship, the Lyric Poetry Prize, a Creative Workforce Fellowship, and the Cleveland Arts Prize. He has worked for peace and justice in the Middle East for over twenty-five years, through a broad range of organizations: Bloomington Coalition for Peace, Committee for Peace in the Middle East, Tikkun, and the Cleveland Nonviolence Network, among others. He is a professor of English and the director of the Peace, Justice, and Human Rights program at John Carroll University.

Lannan Literary Selections

For two decades Lannan Foundation has supported the publication and distribution of exceptional literary works. Copper Canyon Press gratefully acknowledges their support.

LANNAN LITERARY SELECTIONS 2020

Mark Bibbins, *13th Balloon*

Victoria Chang, *Obit*

Leila Chatti, *Deluge*

Philip Metres, *Shrapnel Maps*

Natalie Shapero, *Popular Longing*

RECENT LANNAN LITERARY SELECTIONS FROM COPPER CANYON PRESS

Sherwin Bitsui, *Dissolve*

Jericho Brown, *The Tradition*

John Freeman, *Maps*

Jenny George, *The Dream of Reason*

Ha Jin, *A Distant Center*

Deborah Landau, *Soft Targets*

Maurice Manning, *One Man's Dark*

Rachel McKibbens, *blud*

Aimee Nezhukumatathil, *Oceanic*

Camille Rankine, *Incorrect Merciful Impulses*

Paisley Rekdal, *Nightingale*

Natalie Scenters-Zapico, *Lima :: Limón*

Frank Stanford, *What About This: Collected Poems of Frank Stanford*

Ocean Vuong, *Night Sky with Exit Wounds*

C.D. Wright, *Casting Deep Shade*

Javier Zamora, *Unaccompanied*

Matthew Zapruder, *Father's Day*

Ghassan Zaqtan (translated by Fady Joudah), *The Silence That Remains*

Poetry is vital to language and living. Since 1972, Copper Canyon Press has published extraordinary poetry from around the world to engage the imaginations and intellects of readers, writers, booksellers, librarians, teachers, students, and donors.

WE ARE GRATEFUL FOR THE MAJOR SUPPORT PROVIDED BY:

THE PAUL G. ALLEN
FAMILY FOUNDATION

Anonymous
Jill Baker and Jeffrey Bishop
Anne and Geoffrey Barker
Donna and Matt Bellew
Diana Broze
John R. Cahill
The Beatrice R. and Joseph A. Coleman Foundation Inc.
The Currie Family Fund
Laurie and Oskar Eustis
Saramel and Austin Evans
Mimi Gardner Gates
Gull Industries Inc. on behalf of William True
The Trust of Warren A. Gummow
Carolyn and Robert Hedin
Bruce Kahn
Phil Kovacevich and Eric Wechsler
Lakeside Industries Inc.
on behalf of Jeanne Marie Lee
Maureen Lee and Mark Busto

TO LEARN MORE ABOUT UNDERWRITING
COPPER CANYON PRESS TITLES,
PLEASE CALL 360-385-4925 EXT. 103

WE ARE GRATEFUL FOR THE MAJOR SUPPORT PROVIDED BY:

Peter Lewis

Ellie Mathews and Carl Youngmann as The North Press

Larry Mawby

Hank Meijer

Jack Nicholson

Petunia Charitable Fund and adviser Elizabeth Hebert

Gay Phinny

Suzie Rapp and Mark Hamilton

Emily and Dan Raymond

Jill and Bill Ruckelshaus

Cynthia Sears

Kim and Jeff Seely

Dan Waggoner

Randy and Joanie Woods

Barbara and Charles Wright

Caleb Young as C. Young Creative

The dedicated interns and faithful volunteers
of Copper Canyon Press

The Chinese character for poetry is made up of two parts:
"word" and "temple." It also serves as pressmark for
Copper Canyon Press.

The poems are set in Adobe Caslon Pro.
Book design and composition by Phil Kovacevich.